From Disk to Hard Copy

From Disk to Hard Copy
Teaching Writing with Computers

James Strickland
Slippery Rock University

Boynton/Cook Publishers
HEINEMANN
Portsmouth, NH

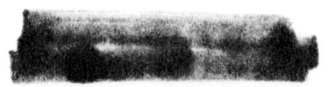

Boynton/Cook Publishers
A subsidiary of Reed Elsevier Inc.
361 Hanover Street
Portsmouth, NH 03801-3912

Offices and agents throughout the world

Copyright © 1997 by James Strickland

All rights reserved. No part of this book may be reproduced in any form or by any electronic or mechanical means, including information storage and retrieval systems, without permission in writing from the publisher, except by a reviewer, who may quote brief passages in a review.

The author and publisher wish to thank those who generously gave permission to reprint borrowed material.

Library of Congress Cataloging-in-Publication Data
Strickland, James.
   From disk to hard copy : teaching writing with computers / James Strickland.
      p. cm.
   Includes bibliographical references and index.
   ISBN 0-86709-416-8 (acid-free paper)
   1. English language--Composition and exercises--Computer-assisted instruction. 2. English language--Composition and exercises--Study and teaching--Data processing. 3. English language--Rhetoric--Study and teaching--Data processing. 4. English language--Rhetoric--Computer assisted instruction. 5. Report writing--Study and teaching--Data processing. 6. Report writing--Computer-assisted instruction. I. Title.
PE1404.S84 1997
808'.042'0785--dc21   96-30019
                                                                                                   CIP

Editor: Peter R. Stillman
Production: Melissa L. Inglis
Cover design: Jenny Jensen Greenleaf
Manufacturing: Louise Richardson

Printed in the United States of America on acid-free paper
00 99 98 97   DA 1 2 3 4 5 6 7 8 9

For Kathleen, forever

Contents

Preface	ix
Introduction	xiii
The Ghost in the Machine	
Teaching Writing with Computers	
One: *Computers, Writing, and Teachers*	1
Integrating Computers into the Classroom	
Budgets and Decision Making	
Equality of Access	
More than Word Processing	
Two: *Helping Students Generate Written Text*	13
Freewriting	
Nutshelling	
Invisible Writing	
Brainstorming	
Devil's Advocate	
Rhetorical Prompts	
Guidance Files	
Collaborative Prewriting	
Finding Out More	
Three: *Helping Students Revise Written Text*	35
Outlining	
Windowing	
Sentence Separation	
Cumulative Sentences	
The Power of Paragraphs	
Conclusions for Introductions	
Collaborative Revision	

Four: *Helping Students Collaborate and Conference*   51
   E-mail Correspondence
   Conferencing
   Comments in the Text
   The Next Step: Networking the Classroom
   Features Common to Network Software
   Posting to a Common Disk
   Modeling Response
   Reading Protocols
   Some Collaborative Assignments

Five: *Helping Students Evaluate and Edit Written Text* 69
   Using Spell Checkers
   Using Style Checkers
   A Minilesson on To Be *Verbs*
   Sentence Separation as Editing Strategy
   Using Search-and-Replace
   Printing and Desktop Publishing
   Collaborative Editing

Six: *The Final Frontier: Cyberspace on the Internet*   85
   Net Addresses
   Inappropriate Material
   Home Pages
   The Credibility Issue
   Research Helpers
   Cyberwriting
   Professional Activity
   Distance Learning
   Conclusion

Appendix A: Glossary of Computer Terms   101
Appendix B: Examples of Representative Software   107
References   117
Index   123

Preface

No matter what you've been told, one of the most difficult things about writing a book is coming up with a title. This book began with the working title *From Disk to Hard Copy*, a title that captured one of the truths my brother, Don, noticed about writing with computers: there are no separate drafts when writing with a computer. Text begins, and what was *prewriting* becomes *revised writing* almost immediately. Writings evolve, growing organically rather than in discrete stages. One student confessed to me that, if his teacher required three drafts and a final copy to be turned in for an assignment, he would simply change a few things on his finished paper and print out three different versions. I wanted a title for my book that would capture this sense of evolving text.

Still, people offered suggestions. Carrie Berger, a student at Big Spring High School in Newville, Pennsylvania, suggested a longer title, *From the Notebook to the Laptop: Teaching During the Classroom Computer Revolution*. Carrie's title reflected the importance that I attached to the teacher's role and the classroom environment. I played with that title in my head, trying to have it sound less like a documentary tracing the history of the revolution. Thank you, Carrie.

Greg Steiger, my son-in-law, offered one of the funniest titles: *The Byte and the Rom Way to Teach English*. As much as I loved it, I was worried that my book would appear too technical with computer jargon in the title. Thank you, Greg. My friend Jeff Golub at the University of South Florida proposed several titles with computer puns. My favorite of Jeff's was, *Scream Savers*. Thank you, Jeff.

Kathleen, my writing partner/life partner, suggested that I do what we did for the title of *Un-Covering the Curriculum*: read the

Preface

manuscript, listening for a recurring phrase. When I did, I discovered how often I stressed the need for collaboration in writing and my sense that writing with a computer supported collaboration—between teacher and student, classmate and classmate, writer and reader. Her title was to be *Collaborative Computing*. Thank you, Kathleen.

In the end, I chose to stay with the original, *From Disk to Hard Copy*, and though some might see that as inflexibility, I like to think of it as trusting one's instincts.

I would like to say a word of thanks to all the composition teachers who were so supportive of each other's work when we were all learning about computers in the early '80s, in particular, Cindy Selfe, Michigan Technological University, and Dawn Rodrigues, then of Colorado State University.

I also want to thank all the wonderful teachers who shared their insights and experiences with me as I was writing this book: Michael Benedict, Fox Chapel High School, PA; Robin Bucaria, Monument Valley High School, UT; Ruth Canham, Kamehameha Schools/Bishop Estate, Honolulu, HI; and Jane Cowden, Big Spring High School, Newville, PA.

Also, Carol Jago, Santa Monica High School; Henry Kiernan, West Morris Regional High School District, NJ; Barbara King-Shaver, South Brunswick High School, NJ; Sandy Lanzoni, Brockway Area High School, PA; Don McAndrew, Indiana University of Pennsylvania; Wanda Porter, Kamehameha Secondary School, Honolulu, HI; Terrie St. Michel, South Mountain High School, Phoenix, AZ; Kathy Simmons, Hempfield Area High School, PA; Don Strickland, Penfield High School, NY; and Herbert Yood, Arlington High School, MA.

I also need to thank some students who were very helpful in letting me see writing with a computer from their point of view: the students at Big Spring High School, including Jillian Bower, Rebecca Chamberlin, Tsiphuneah Grosso, Katie Smith, and Jessica Watson; and the students at Hempfield Area High School, including Philip Andrews, Nicole Angelicchio, Carolyn Baker, Jamie Sue Crouse, Kelly Dzendzel, Heather Lambing, Justin

Marinos, Diane Persin, Kristi Romas, Katie Stewart, and Amber Stuver.

Thanks are also owed to Laurie Morrison, Ann Wallace, and Tracy Wallace, Slippery Rock University; and Ken Strickland, Penfield High School.

I would like to express a special thanks to Peter Stillman, senior editor at Boynton/Cook, who is, without a doubt, a writer's editor. Peter spends his time with his writers in genuine conversation about their particular book's philosophical orientation, pedagogical approach, and general right-mindedness. The first time I met Peter was in 1983 when we were both presenting at the New York State English Council conference on Long Island, at which I was sharing my ideas for the first time about teaching writing with computers. I'm happy to say he's been supportive of my work, directly and indirectly, ever since then.

Heinemann is fortunate to have many talented people in their employ. I would like to express my gratitude to one person in particular, Melissa Inglis—Kathleen and I rely on her judgment and advice.

Finally, I can never fully express how much of my writing is owed to Kathleen. I thank her for her facilitative support, her collaboration, and her love.

Introduction

The Ghost in the Machine

I first became involved with computers in 1981 when I took a continuing education course to learn programming on the relatively new Apple II, writing instructions in BASIC (a computer language whose acronym stands for Beginner's All-Purpose Symbolic Instruction Code). My earliest programs were simple multiple-choice quizzes in which the computer presented a question with possible answers on screen, waited for a response, checked the response against an answer key, gave feedback concerning the correctness of the response, and kept track of the number of correct responses. To me, this was the dawn of interactive computing.

Because I am an English teacher, I began applying my fledgling computer skills to developing a writing program to prompt writers in 1982. Instead of asking quiz questions, I programmed the personal computer to ask prewriting prompts, the importance of which had been suggested by Richard Young's "Paradigms and Problems" (1978) and Ross Winterowd's *Contemporary Rhetoric* (1975). After some early attempts, I read that Hugh Burns (1980) had pioneered the computers for composition movement with his programs written in 1977 for mainframe computers at the University of Texas at Austin. I was pleased to meet Hugh Burns at the 1983 Conference on College Composition and Communication in Detroit. He was encouraging about my work and predicted that computers would prove to be very helpful to writers.

Over the next few years, I developed two computer prewriting programs: QUEST, a program of guided writing prompts, and

Introduction

FREE, a freewriting program. QUEST would help writers by asking them direct questions about their writing; FREE would help by indirectly guiding them in a series of freewriting and synthesis cycles, modeled on the work of Peter Elbow (1973). Computer programs that would mimic the helpful probes and prods of a sympathetic writing teacher were attempted by other composition teachers, such as Dawn and Ray Rodrigues (1983), Michael Spitzer (1984), Mimi Schwartz (1982), Helen Schwartz (1984), Cindy Selfe and Billie Wahlstrom (1983), and Ruth Von Blum and Michael Cohen (1984).

At that time, I believed that a computer-assisted guided heuristic such as QUEST would prove to be the most helpful to writers, even though the computer had difficulty responding to the writers, treating the topic and the responses as meaningless strings of words to be assigned places in "slot-and-fill" blanks left in sentences. When I discovered that writers seemed to find freewriting more helpful (Strickland 1987), I faulted my computer program. I kept rewriting the code for QUEST, trying to make the program more sophisticated, offering more branching options to handle the variety of responses entered by writers, and asking more questions tailored to the specific writing topics and tasks. Although I was pleased that QUEST won the Assembly for Computers in English (ACE) Best Shareware Software Award in 1988, the program became so unwieldy that by 1989 I stopped developing it. No matter how much work was done by writing teachers like myself trying to make these programs perform as intelligent tutors, the computer could not simulate human response without human understanding. A teacher and a computer can both respond to a student's writing with a comment as simple as, "Tell me more," but only the teacher, as a real reader, would be able to tie the response to the content, saying, "I was interested in hearing more about . . ."

I studied Artificial Intelligence (AI), hoping to create a computer program that would act as an intelligent tutor, prompting writers the way that a teacher or a peer-tutor might. I learned AI languages with exotic names such as LISP, WALTZ, and PRO-

LOG, but I found the breakthroughs were occurring in fields such as medicine, engineering, and circuit diagnosis. A human writing tutor, on the other hand, was difficult to simulate; AI applications done with writing were limited to parsing sentences and locating grammar errors. Again, I was at a loss as to how the computer could be helpful to writers and teachers of writing.

It became apparent that computer programmers must find a way for the computer to respond to the ways writers represent their knowledge and to understand the ways ideas are expressed before computers can hope to simulate the behavior and expert knowledge of human tutors, what Burns (1984) calls "rhetorical services." Until these obstacles are overcome, computer-assisted instruction will be slot-and-fill programming, ghosts in the machine masquerading as "intelligent" agents, soon unmasked by students, who remark as one of my students did when she realized that the computer was giving her canned responses, "Oh, I see how this works" (Strickland 1989).

Teaching Writing with Computers

This is not a computer book; it is a writing book. It is designed to help teachers use computers to support writers, offering strategies that would be impossible or unlikely without the technology. This is not a book for techies, modem monsters, computer lizards, or nerds. This book will apply what we know of composition theory to the use of computers in the writing classroom.

This book will support students as they use the computer to generate material. It will encourage notions spun in electronic text, guided by classical and modern rhetorical invention strategies, ideas that create meaning in the act of writing itself.

In class, a student might interpret a teacher's comment to add more details as "add more adjectives," while the teacher was thinking more along the lines of "expand the description and elaborate more." This book will suggest ways of using the computer environment to revise or re-imagine texts.

Introduction

Students are often most anxious about the correctness of their writing—spelling, grammar, punctuation, word choice. This book will help teachers suggest ways students can make sense of the wealth of information that word processing editing functions give concerning surface features of their writing, while still ensuring that student writers retain control over their text and its meaning.

Writing is more than the solitary act of an individual composing at a computer. This book will help teachers and students collaborate and conference with each other in the classroom and over a network. Many teachers will want to have their students write to each other and to students or adults outside the classroom; in short, they will want what the Internet provides. This book will demystify the mysteries of cyberspace and suggest ways to use networking to promote better writing.

In the fifteen years since I began studying the teaching of writing with computers, I found that I had been mistakenly thinking of the computer as an actor in the learning environment; I needed to think of the computer as a part of the learning environment itself. My quest changed from trying to develop the perfect piece of software to thinking about how to use the writing software available—primarily word processing—to allow writers to do what writers do: generate material, manipulate that material after reviewing, confer and collaborate with others, edit their documents, and publish a final copy. This book, then, is the fulfillment of that quest.

Chapter One

Computers, Writing, and Teachers

Teachers want their students to be excited about learning and many feel that computers will do the trick. As Jeff Golub (1996) says, "Turn on your computers; turn on your students!" Teachers are excited about computers because they feel that word processing takes the drudgery out of rewriting a paper, making otherwise illegible handwritten papers easier to read. They also know that knowledge of computers is required for the future. Yet some teachers still approach the computer as little more than an expensive electronic typewriter, a machine that makes easily corrected, neatly typed papers. Others regard the computer as a powerful entity in the classroom, an alchemist's stone capable of transforming everything it touches. I'm suggesting that the computer is somewhere in between: it is more than a tool and less than a god.

To receive the maximum benefit from computer technology, teachers need to think about the computer's place in a student-centered classroom. Teachers need to see the computer as a machine that can help their students solve their writing problems—getting ideas, generating text, manipulating that text after reviewing, collaborating with others in the classroom or over a network, editing their documents, and finally publishing hard copy—but it will not magically transform them. This book can help teachers use computers to support writers, offering strategies that would be impossible or unlikely without the technology.

Integrating Computers into the Classroom

Terrie St. Michel (1996), a teacher at South Mountain High School in Arizona, confesses that "for all my comfort and experience with computers, I was reluctant to integrate them into my classroom" (1). Terrie perceived the time her students spent in the library's computer lab as little more than "a loss of class time" (1). After all, she didn't think it unreasonable to expect her students to practice keyboarding and "type" their assignments on their own time. Furthermore, she had trouble considering the lab an English classroom when the writing materials—textbooks, dictionaries, handouts, and other resources—were all back in the classroom.

Barbara King-Shaver (1996) says that many English teachers at South Brunswick High School, New Jersey, sign up to take whole classes to the computer lab, where there are twenty-five new computers (the lab gets new equipment before individual classrooms). Unfortunately, use of the lab is not uniform. Some take their students once every other week, some rarely at all. Perhaps the tedium of reserving the lab in advance, never having enough printers, students knowing different word processing programs, losing files, reloading programs, and saving files gets in the way, making teachers hesitant to give up their valuable class time.

Many have felt this concern about losing class time to the computer. My department has been arguing about how much class time should be spent in the computer lab. Some of my colleagues suspect the students' desire to go to the lab is a way to do homework during class time. Others say that this interpretation has more to do with our sense that a written assignment is work to be completed at home rather than an interactive enterprise that best takes place within a community of learners. One of Robin Bucaria's (1996) students at Monument Valley High School in Utah, who is working hard at writing, revising, and learning to edit on the computer, commented, "English is fun. All we do is come to class and play around on computers." It isn't always easy for students or teachers to overcome these preconceived notions.

Out of the Lab and into the Classroom

Terrie St. Michel (1996) has an entirely different attitude now that the computers are in her own classroom, saying, "What has endeared me to using computers has been the added flexibility their presence offers" (2). During her writing workshop classes, her students are free to write on any of the ten computers available, read independently, engage in peer conferencing, or any other related activity.

Jane Cowden (1996) finds that students in her reader/writer workshop classes at Big Spring High School in Newville, Pennsylvania, make maximum use of the three computers she has in the back of her classroom (discarded and contributed by the military). Barbara King-Shaver reports the same activity in English classrooms that have up to four computers (discarded by their technology lab). Jane's students take turns, three days a week, and frequently two or three will pull chairs up to one computer and work together. Although Jane leaves the choice of using the computer up to the student, she has observed that those who use the computers are writing more and are more likely to revise than those who do not. Terrie St. Michel regards the fact that her students "seem to be more interested in working on their writings when they are able to use computers" (3) as the greatest advantage to having the technology in her classroom. Barbara King-Shaver says South Brunswick students will enjoy four to five new computers in each English classroom when they move to a new building in 1997. Ann Heide and Dale Henderson (1994) see placing as few as three or four computers in the classroom as freeing the school's computer lab for other functions. "Rather than being a room where students go to 'do' computer for a period of time, [a school computer lab can be] used for introducing new software, for direct instruction . . . and for allowing greater access to students as they explore and try out new software" (15).

J. P. Shaver (1990) found that high-ability students appreciate the computer's ability to help them do better what they already do well, while the low-ability students, now able to take risks without embarrassment, enjoy the computer's error-spotting and revising aids and its neat printouts. Regardless of ability, students rarely pronounce themselves computer experts. Katie Stewart, a student at Hempfield Area High School in Pennsylvania, still considers herself "a bit computer illiterate" even though she knows how to "log on, type a paper, spell check it, save it, open it at a later time." Katie has a sense that computers have powers that exceed her understanding. Sandra Lanzoni (1996), a teacher at Brockway Area Junior/Senior High School in Pennsylvania, explains the confusion about being computer literate and being able to use the computer as a misconception about the nature of writing with a computer by saying that students "have experience with computers and sometimes with word processing, [but] they do not seem to have much experience with drafting on computers." Another Hempfield student, Nicole Angelicchio, confesses that she doesn't know any computer strategies for writing, although she types, revises, edits, and checks spelling and grammar on the computer. Perhaps it is the experience of *creating* on the computer that escapes these students, since many teachers have them begin by typing longhand versions of their assignments to save time in the lab/classroom.

Students are grateful for the chance to use computers. Terrie St. Michel allows even students from other classes to use the computers during their free periods, finding it "relatively nondisruptive to what my other students are doing" (3). Carol Jago (1995), a teacher at Santa Monica High School in California, allows students to use her computers whenever the machines are free, to use her paper supply, and to ask for help when they have trouble (regardless of whether the students are hers). Carol doesn't worry about security. Her students "shut down the machines, cover them, turn out the lights, and even empty the trash. In seven years, no student has ever trashed anything of [hers] or sabotaged another student's work" (3). A note left in an anonymous file on the hard disk thanked her by saying, "Sometimes I think about all the paper I have wasted printing copies of things I have not really proofread. I must owe Mrs. Jago a case of paper. I come in here without even asking and am never questioned. When I have trouble, the teacher is happy to fix the printer quickly and efficiently (without even knowing who I am). I feel like I owe something to this teacher or this room, considering that my life, meaning my future in college and everything else I do for school, depends on whether or not I can use the computer" (2–3).

Of course, with computers, students no longer have an excuse for not getting their assignments typed, but other disasters await them. Herbert Yood (1996), a teacher at Arlington High School in Massachusetts, promotes what he calls "defensive computering," stridently urging students to save their work on at least two diskettes, refusing to accept disk failure as an excuse for an incomplete assignment.

Budgets and Decision Making

Whenever teachers gather, everyone seems to have a story about how decisions about computers in the classroom were made or influenced by someone in administration, someone in another department, or by persons from some outside interest group—parents, community agencies, the federal government—and rarely by the teachers themselves. Why is there so much interference? Why are people other than teachers making the decisions about the academic use of computers? One answer is that computers require an investment of resources—a new budget line—that classroom programs never received previously, especially writing classrooms: additional staff are needed (faculty and aides knowledgeable about computers must be hired or provided with appropriate retraining), service contracts must be made, software must be purchased or developed, and supplies must be ordered. Computers haven't created the paperless environment; if anything, students are more willing to print multiple copies of whatever draft they're working on. This means increased expenses for computer supplies: reams of printer paper, toner cartridges for laser printers, ribbons/ink cartridges for older printers, and disks for individual and back-up use.

A minor budget crisis occurred in our department's writing lab when, several weeks before the end of the term, a student designed a promotional flyer for her student government campaign on a school computer. Her eye-catching flyer featured white lettering on a black background. She would have used a whole ream of paper if the printer hadn't quit around 300 copies. Her creative black background had entirely depleted the toner cartridge. Of course, there was no money in the budget to purchase another cartridge until the next academic year, and the crisis occurred just before hundreds of students were expected to arrive to print their final research papers. Someone's budget had to pay for the cartridge, which meant involving administrators, who are often unwilling to trust teachers to make appropriate decisions, that is, management decisions.

Public schools are under pressure to prepare students for the technology of the future, but the ones charged with these preparations are too often those who have little understanding of the pedagogical applications of computers, which results in poor management. For example, attempting to deal with what they see as a noise/distraction problem, administrators may redesign computer rooms to isolate writers from each other, and in doing so, may architecturally impede collaborative learning. Our computer lab was designed by managers concerned with electrical supply lines and table space. They had no interest in creating a computer room designed for interaction among authors, texts, readers, and teachers. Another example of poor management is the policy that our computer labs function without outside service contracts, which results in anywhere from one to three machines or even a printer out of order on any given day. Administrators accept this occurrence; teachers and students must not. Teachers using computers need to become proactive in a way that they have never had to before. Teachers need to approach management as the experts, able to make cost-sensitive suggestions and explain their needs in terms of sound pedagogical practice. Teachers need to see that being informed about technology does not mean they give up their status as English teachers to become media specialists. Today's English teacher makes many informed choices about the classroom, including decisions concerning what literature to teach, what textbooks to use, what pedagogy to follow, and how to integrate computers in the classroom.

Equality of Access

Today, most schools, knowing the fiscal impossibility of expecting each student to have his or her own computer in class, use lab setups as the most equitable allocation of resources. Some schools still give business and science classes priority scheduling for the computer labs, but this is not as common as it was ten years ago. Most are convinced of the need for English teachers to have access to computers, if only to have students use word processing. Henry Kiernan, a former English teacher now an administrator, says, "We no longer have turf rooms such as a *Math Lab* or a *Writing Center* [at West Morris High School, New Jersey]—every room is connected to the local-area network (LAN), and every computer connected to the LAN can be used by any teacher. [The change] has been transformational."

It would be naive to believe that computers will be available for everyone in the same way. The potential for technology should be democratic, international, and culturally transcendent; however, the reality is that home computers belong to members of first world nations who are predominantly white and economically advantaged, and computers are therefore more readily available to their children and the schools their children attend.

Students who have computers at home will have an additional advantage by being able to do more of what they can already do in school. As school districts race to out-distance each other in terms of technology, the greater the gap will be between the

Chapter One Computers, Writing, and Teachers

computer "haves" and "have-nots." The "haves" in our society will always have the latest hardware and software, and our only hope is to ensure the "have nots" have access in school. While we might not be able to change the inequality of access, perhaps teachers can find a way to be as effective as possible with the computers they have available for students during the school day.

When I was in high school, I was on our swim team. The problem was that our small parochial school didn't have a swimming pool for us to practice in. We had to use the public school's pool, practicing at times that were convenient for the public school. We never won a competition, but we did compete. Outside school, there's not much we can do about inequalities. It is my hope that those who lack at-home computers can make maximum use of the facilities available during class time and after-school.

Terrie St. Michel (1996) believes that her district is committed to technology. "All [ninth grade] English classes spend at least a week in the computer lab where they receive orientation on how to use the computers and various software programs.... Computers are scattered throughout the campus and students use them in their social studies, science, [special] magnet [courses], and foreign language classes in addition to their English, math, and business classes. Students can use computers for doing research, writing, editing, and formalizing their work. Many students have computers at home and use computers at their [after-school] jobs" (4).

Within the same classes at Hempfield Area High School, Kathy Simmons finds students who have home computers with CD-ROM capability and Internet access, while others have no computer and must use the computers in her homeroom. Herbert Yood (1996) finds that access and ability to use computers at Arlington High School correlate with academic standing and economics. A greater percentage of students in the more advanced sections of English have computers at home. Their equipment is newer and more sophisticated than what the public schools can offer. They prefer to use their computers at home and need little instruction.

One Hempfield student, Carolyn Baker, admits that she "usually refuses to use the ones installed by [her] school.... School computers run slowly and they lack . . . capabilities [such as a CD-ROM reader] and features that mine has, features I have grown accustomed to, and depend on." This division between home computing and school computing deprives students such as Carolyn of the opportunity to learn strategies that they wouldn't discover on their own—generating material, revising, and editing—and the chance to use computers to confer and to collaborate.

Students in the "lower-level" classes at Arlington High School, who have had little success with writing, are less likely to have computers at home, says Herbert Yood (1996). For these students, public education is their only chance to acquire computer skills. The challenge to teachers such as Terrie St. Michel, Kathy Simmons, and Herbert Yood is to help *all* students find something useful and educational in a computer experience in school. By fostering a collaborative atmosphere in class, teachers can enlist computer-advantaged students such as Carolyn as mentors for the computer-deprived. And Carolyn will receive something she couldn't get at home, alone with her computer—support from her classmates as they use the computer to confer with her, Carolyn the writer. Students who have computers in the classroom will benefit not only from the technology itself but from the strategies and the collaboration that their teachers actively promote.

More than Word Processing

If, as mentioned earlier, the computer is more than a tool, then we must acknowledge that the computer is not value-neutral and that it privileges certain behaviors and ways of thinking (McAndrew 1995). First, it privileges conceiving of writing as a collection of word processing functions. When Kathy Simmons

(1996) asked her students at Hempfield to discuss the strategies they use when writing with computers, the overwhelming majority of students described the word processing functions they used, notably the spell checking and thesaurus/ grammar features. Sandra Lanzoni (1996) argues a difficulty distinguishing drafting from word processing: "writing with computers is more than word processing functions." Though teachers can use the computer to support prewriting, the invention stage of writing is not represented by any function of word processing. Word processing also tends to equate revision with copy-editing, though it is able to support both aspects of the writing process. Word processing makes no allowances for novice writers; all of its features are offered to every writer the same.

And yet, word processing can make a significant contribution to having writers conceive of the writing process as fluid and ever-changing. Writing with a pen/paper or typewriter tends to promote "carved in stone" thinking about writing. Changes that are made to pen/paper or typewriter copies usually mean the physical destruction of the copy. Real writers can't help but cross out, start over, and move things around, and a computer's word processing facilitates this activity. Only a few keystrokes are needed to delete, copy, move, and rearrange text. Unlike the crossouts and arrows so evident when using a pen/paper or typewriter, the altered text on a computer copy neither looks messy nor requires recopying. When word processing, nothing is permanent until a printed copy—hard copy—is generated, and expert writers tell us that they judge their comfort with the machine by how long they can resist the urge to get a printout. So, writing is different from word processing, but word processing supports writers. The issue is whether the computer lets writers create in ways they couldn't or wouldn't otherwise.

The technology also promotes conceiving of classroom interaction as occurring between one individual user and one machine. Just when teachers have gotten their students away from the "desks in rows, eyes forward, no talking allowed" model of the classroom, technology entices them to the computer lab/classroom, placing students once again in rows (across the room or along the walls) looking forward at a screen, not talking to anyone else. In a less-than-random sampling of teachers from across the country, I've found the dominant model for the layout of computers in classrooms is lined up against the back of the room, along a side wall, or, if there are enough machines, on tables in rows so the students can look over the monitors at the teacher in the front of the room. Just when teachers have convinced students that they are more than individuals working to get individual assignments done, that they are part of a writing community, collaborating on drafts, sharing their journals, giving feedback to each other, technology has them working alone at their own computer, acknowledging those near them only when they have to share a printer.

Teachers need to encourage students to talk when using the computer, or whisper if the noise becomes distracting. When everything is displayed openly on computer screens, teachers need to demonstrate respect for another's privacy while encouraging students to invite their teacher and classmates to read what is displayed. When students are confused about what button to push, teachers have to resist the temptation to be the class problem-solver, making the students responsible in an atmosphere of mutual aid. Teachers shouldn't abandon the "process" approach to writing that they've worked hard to get middle school and high school students to adopt. Teachers who use composition theory to drive their instruction have now only to add the component of computers to use that same composition theory to benefit from technology in the writing classroom. Teachers in a computer writing environment can still teach strategies that will help students keep the flow going, writing in a collaborative setting, reaching out to audiences other than the teacher, publishing desktop documents and exploring nontraditional forms of writing. As Carol Jago (1995) says, "For me, [computers bring a] shift in student attitude that marks a classroom power shift. [The classroom is] not *theirs* or *mine*, its *ours*" (3).

Chapter Two

Helping Students Generate Written Text

Consider how cavalierly teachers give their students writing assignments, directing each to take knowledge from various sources, synthesize it and thereby create meaning, in effect, asking for an explicit understanding of a situation or event where none existed previously.

Yet no matter how many times teachers make assignments and students respond in writing, nothing is potentially more frightening to a writer than a blank page. At the moment when pen touches page, many writers have a terrible fear of making a false move, writing the wrong thing, or making a bad start. When writing with a word processing program, that same fear exists, even though conventional wisdom would predict that a computer's ability to delete anything that isn't quite right would be liberating, especially since cross-outs and erasures are undetectable. But I have found that this potential to erase and rewrite makes some writers even more nervous. I've had students spend almost an entire class period trying to get the first sentence right, typing a tentative beginning, backspacing, typing an alternative, deleting a word or two, and finally erasing the entire line. A more productive strategy would be to participate in an uninhibited generation of text, withholding judgment as to its suitability until later. The secret to writing is to begin.

The trick to starting is to just start, without worrying about making false steps, knowing everything is correctable and changeable—later. In short, "generate-then-judge." Unfortunately, some students have learned to monitor their output to such a degree that they are never quite willing to withhold judgment. Delayed judgment can benefit from what cognitive psychologists call an incubation effect: when writers return their text, their writing is seen in a new light. Writing with computers can help convince students that it's all right to make a mess and clean it up later.

Freewriting

When writing with a computer, students can use a number of techniques to help with the uninhibited generation of text, the heart of the "generate-then-judge" strategy. The most obvious technique is freewriting, a non-directive prewriting strategy in which students are invited to write as quickly as they can, allowing their minds to jump from one idea to the next as quickly as the connections are suggested. Our minds work on the principle of association, and freewriting takes advantage of the chaotic connections that one's subconscious mind makes, leaping from one thought to the next, often without making explicit the reason for the connection.

When freewriting, one restrains concerns about grammar, punctuation, coherence, or a grade. A writer simply writes. But freewriting is hardly a computer strategy, is it? When it was popularized by Peter Elbow (1973), freewriting was embraced as a way to reach the reluctant writer, a way to free the writer from constraints. Some teachers I know refer to freewriting as making a "sloppy copy," countering the temptation to erase errors and to be cautious of what is committed to ink, combating the desire for perfection. Oddly enough, a computer rarely makes a "sloppy copy," although it does allow the freedom of expression that is central to freewriting simply because the draft can be cleaned up without any trace of the chaos. Freewriting with a computer encourages a free flow of words on the screen—words easily correctable, easily expendable, and easily rearranged if not in quite the right order.

The procedure for freewriting with a computer is pretty much the same as it is without computers. Students are directed to begin to write whatever comes to mind about their subject (or even their lack of a subject). If they get stuck, they are directed simply to write that they are stuck:

> . . . and now I cannot think of anything else to say, so I guess I'm stuck, I wonder what will get me unstuck, like the time I was stuck in the snow, that was coming home after a basketball game . . .

At some point, the mind will leap to another topic. The stipulation for writers using the computer is the constraint not to go back with the delete key, the backspace key, or even the left arrow key. Writers are simply directed to write. They should write until the screen is completely full. That's about five minutes for me. It might take some students ten minutes. Once they fill the screen, ask them to stop at the end of the sentence and get a printout. This will allow students to see what they've written in a different form—hard copy, as computer-printed text has come to be called. Freewriting with a computer has the further advantage of storing each of the writings on a disk, to be recalled later as students search for topics of personal interest to write about. English teachers at the Kamehameha schools in Hawaii are teaching students to view computers as places to store memories, notes, and ideas to be recovered later for writing, just as storytellers rehearse ideas in their mind or replay memories (Porter 1996). The students are taught that storing information in a computer file eliminates the burden of having to remember everything they wanted to write or ideas that might not be useful at the moment but are worth preserving.

Nutshelling

Once students are familiar with freewriting on the computer, they can begin some variations. One sometimes neglected aspect of Elbow's freewriting is his sense that writers need to pull together what they've written—a synthesis stage he calls finding "the center of gravity" (35). Elbow realized that freewriting is unpredictable. So, from time to time writers need to try a technique known as nutshelling to give direction to their writing (Flower 1985). Nutshelling is tied to the expression, "that's it in a nutshell," meaning, that's it in brief. I suppose the expression comes from the difficulty people have of cracking open a nutshell, and the delight they experience in finding the meat of the nut inside.

When teachers direct their students to apply the strategy of nutshelling to writing, they follow a period of freewriting with a one-sentence summary that captures the most interesting idea(s) found after rereading what was written. This one-sentence summary contains the essence of the freewriting episode—in a nutshell—tight, compact, and all meat. I tell students to try to write a sentence that captures the most interesting item or idea that they came up with in their freewriting.

Obviously, nutshelling is not a computer-intensive writing strategy. Yet the computer can provide a useful alternative. Instead of having students write a nutshell sentence, teachers can ask their students to review their freewritings, searching for a nutshell sentence. If they find one, they can use the copy/move sequence of the word processing program to reproduce the sentence at the end of the freewriting, where the duplicate will serve as the one-sentence summary.

Those who are unable to find a suitable sentence can be challenged to write one. And those who are stuck for what to write can be asked to complete either of these prompts: "I guess what I was trying to say was . . ." and "What surprised me most in reading what I had written was . . ."

Nutshelling supplies a judgment aspect for the "generate-then-judge" strategy. No matter how far one's thoughts have wandered from the original topic, or how stuck one has become, nutshelling provides a strategy for starting over and refocusing a piece of writing. For example, when I freewrite, I am surprised at not only just how far my mind can wander, but also at the great ideas I just might stumble upon. If I'm writing about Italy, my mind might begin to think of pizza (even while knowing the pizza pie is an American creation, not an Italian dish). When I think of pizza, I get hungry, and begin to think of going to Pizza Joe's, but then I think of someone I met there the last time I went to pick up a pizza.

OK, that's quite normal, but then my mind begins to run through associations of people and pizza, certainly without my asking it to. And I suddenly remember Oscar, a guy I knew twenty-five years ago. I was walking to the television room in the dorm, and this guy came in carrying a pizza. He looked at me, looked at the pizza he carried, turned to me and asked if I'd like some. I was shocked; I was never offered pizza by a stranger. He must have noticed the confused look on my face because he explained that we were in the same English class. From that my mind races on to remember the odd professor who taught the class that my pizza friend and I took together.

All this and I thought I was writing about Italy. See? If it were really important that I write about Italy, I could just start over. However, if I'm on a free discovery journey, I can use nutshelling.

I could write:

I'll never forget the friendship that began with a pizza.

or

I must've looked hungry because he offered me a pizza and he became a friend.

or

I don't know what I liked better—the offer of pizza or the offer of friendship.

The nutshell sentence can later be recycled, thanks to the computer's copy/move sequence, to act as an opening sentence or a concluding sentence, either for the paragraph, the section, or the entire essay.

From this one-sentence nutshell summary, I direct my students to start freewriting again, using an alternating cycle of freewriting-nutshelling-freewriting. The cycle of creating and synthesizing can continue until a writer runs out of ideas or runs out of time. But I suggest writing a final nutshell; it seems to put closure on the experience.

Invisible Writing

What can teachers do for students who can't fight the temptation to go back and reread while freewriting, checking for errors and thinking instead of typing? Some rereading is natural to the writing process, but when freewriting doesn't seem to work, even with nutshelling, then teachers might suggest a strategy to compensate for the risk-taking that other students seem to feel comfortable doing. For those who seem overly distracted by the text produced so far, the solution is to not look. This is easier said than done, unless one's students are writing with a computer. The computer's television-type display of text on screen is the key to this strategy. For those who can't help looking back at what they've produced, rethinking what they just wrote, simply turn off the screen. The first to advocate this technique, calling it *invisible writing*, was Stephen Marcus (1984; 1991), presently the Associate Director of a National Writing Project affiliate at the University of California at Santa Barbara. Marcus (1991) suggested turning down the brightness of the screen so students cannot see what they've written, to temporarily "hide" text while students brainstorm (9). Invisible writing will help students focus on the content of their writing instead of its surface features; it will "build fluency by freeing students from the common desire to interrupt their prewriting to 'tinker' with their words" (9). Marcus warns students their fingers will strike the wrong keys, words will be horribly misspelled, sentences won't make sense, and grammar will be nonstandard. But he promises his students that the frustration will be worth it, their creativity heightened.

I have a computer monitor with a separate on/off switch that accomplishes the same thing. I get the feeling of writing with my eyes closed or blindfolded; I can only do it for so long before I just have to look. And this looking back may be not only necessary but also instructive, showing students how rereading stimulates thought and directs cohesive writing.

When students turn the brightness control back up, they may find they have written something on the screen that looks like this:

> I kdon;t know what to write I think I have to pay my tuition this week or else theyll concel my classes msybe I could write about that it if students didnt hav eto wrok to pay the hgi tuition they could study moreI;lll write about the problems of students are getting wripped off on the fees and tuition being changerd.

Obviously there are punctuation mistakes, typos, and grammatical errors, notably a fused sentence, yet the invisible writing generated some workable content, text that can be easily corrected by deleting the excess and fixing the errors, allowing what appears on the screen to be changed to:

> Students are being ripped off by the fees and excessive tuition being charged and the consequence is that they have to spend their time working to pay for their studies instead of working at their studies.

Of course, the same freewriting done on paper would require a clean sheet of paper to copy over the worthwhile ideas, but what is more important, this freewriting might never have been generated at all, had it been started on paper or with the computer screen set to normal brightness. Nonetheless, this technique comes with a caution. Since writers naturally rely on what they have written so far as a stimulus to what they'll write next, invisible writing is not offered as a way to teach writing, as some critics have suggested. Invisible writing is merely a creativity booster, to be used when students feel their internal editor stifling their creativity (Blau 1983).

Marcus (1991) suggests alternating visible and invisible writing in bursts of 2–5 minutes. The nutshelling strategy can be used by lightening the screen after an invisible freewriting session and, after reading what had been typed, a nutshell sentence could be written in response to prompts such as, "What do I want my reader to care about at this point?" and "What am I worried about in my writing right now?" (Marcus 1991, 10). Alternatively, the screen could be darkened after a visible writing session to write a nutshell sentence in the invisible mode.

Brainstorming

I'm sure most teachers have used brainstorming, an idea-generating technique whereby students call out or write down ideas as quickly as they come. Brainstorming is much like freewriting, except the ideas are not even preformed into sentences; these ideas usually come out looking like a grocery list, items written down on the sheet of paper but not in any particular order. When students use the brainstormed ideas to draft their text, they might imagine themselves shopping for ideas. When one uses a grocery list, the items are crossed off as they are found on the shelf in the store. When brainstorming, writers might cross the ideas off as they are used in the writing. Sometimes writers prefer to reorganize the list before beginning to write the draft, numbering the order in which the ideas are to be dealt with. When using paper and pen, brainstorming involves not only generating the ideas but a great deal of crossing out, drawing arrows, and adding sequencing numbers. The result can often be a mess. When brainstorming on the computer, the ideas can be reorganized (using the copy/move sequence) and deleted (using the delete key or the block/delete sequence). The result is the same, without the mess: the brainstormed ideas judged useful are re-sequenced and the ideas judged inappropriate are removed. The rearrangement can be repeated and even become an ongoing process.

Students can be directed to examine the list to see what sort of order is suggested. One student might notice that the list seems to involve a time sequence, things happening in a "first, then, and then" pattern. Another student might sense that some items are the causes of a group of other items. The items might divide into "part of the problem" and "part of the solution." The brainstormed items may be parts inside of other parts, a microcosm/macrocosm effect like what one gets with the Ukrainian wooden dolls that open in the middle to reveal another doll, one size smaller, hidden inside.

For example, Ann Wallace, a student of mine at Slippery Rock University, took her brainstormed list of ideas (see Figure 2-1), and using the copy/move sequence, organized the items according to the categories it suggested (see Figure 2-2).

After completing this stage of brainstorming, what remains is a clean, organized plan to follow in writing the draft. The plan from the brainstorming session can be included as notes or as part of the draft itself. Writers can use the windowing feature to create two separate work spaces on the computer screen, placing

Married Names

 take husband's
 keep maiden name
 hyphenate
 children's names?
 choose a different name
 husband takes wife's
 foreign names mispronounced
 woman's right to choose
 husband's right to choose
 parents' right to impose choice
 society's right to impose choice
 government's right to impose choice
 tradition
 ownership
 unity as couple
 credit problems
 self-perception?
 already established socially
 already established financially

Figure 2-1 Original Brainstormed List

21

Married Names

Options a woman has when choosing a married name:
Wife takes the husband's last name
Wife keeps maiden name
Wife hyphenates her last name with her husband's
    maiden name-husband's name
    husband's name-maiden name
Husband takes the wife's last name
Wife and husband together choose a different name

Reasons why women choose the last name that they use:
Tradition
Name well-established in the community
Taking the husband's last name denotes ownership
To show unity between husband and wife
Husband has bad credit/wife has better credit
Foreign-sounding names are often mispronounced

Who has the right to choose the woman's last name:
The woman
The husband
His parents
Her parents
Society
Government

What difference will it make:
How does last name affect the children?
If a woman is well established socially/financially by a certain
    name, what impact will the name change have on her?
How does a woman's last name change her self-perception?
What name do the children use if the woman chooses a name
    other than that of her husband?

Figure 2-2 Organized List by Suggested Categories

the outline file or a brainstorming list in one window, displaying the actual text-in-progress in the other window.

Another way that writers use brainstorming is to construct a map or model by drawing trees, clusters, webs, and diagrams. Just as a tree appears as one large stem, branching off into two, three, or four major stalks, each of those breaking out as smaller branches, ideas generated for a writing can be organized that way. The topic can be broken into two, three, or four major components, each of which consists of separate elements and so forth. The tree is usually drawn upside-down with the main branch at the top of the page with lines coming off it, representing the branches. Clustering involves a non-hierarchical grouping of ideas. As ideas are generated in the brainstorming sessions, they are grouped with the ideas that are similar. Webs are similar to trees in that they make explicit the connection between ideas, yet they differ from trees because there is no implied linear progression from major to minor ideas (see Figure 2-3). Diagrams, like the Venn diagrams used in mathematical sets and logic problems, use the clustering approach to group

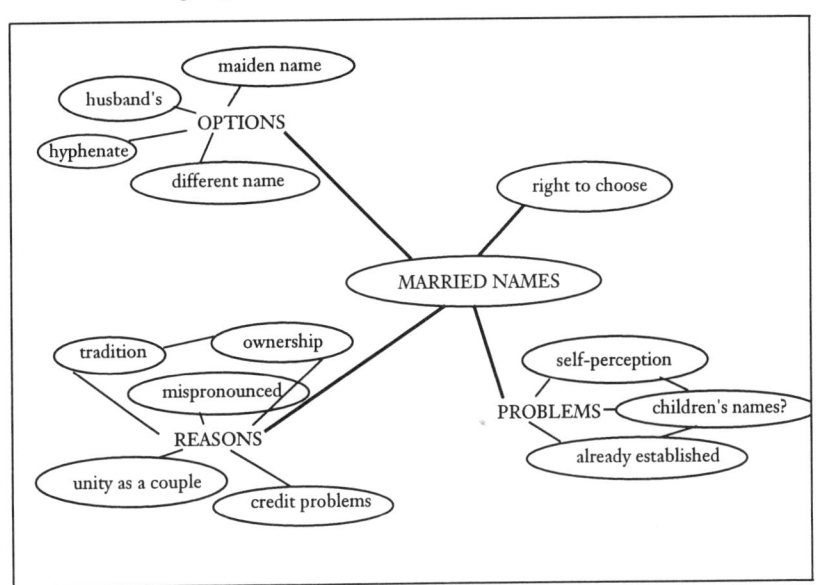

Figure 2-3 Brainstormed List as a Web

ideas and also a series of interlocking circles to indicate where ideas have areas of shared concerns.

Some computer programs, such as INSPIRATION used at South Brunswick High School in New Jersey, include graphics programs that allow writers to link ideas by drawing lines and to group ideas by drawing circles to contain corresponding ideas (see Appendix B). If a program with this type of feature is not available, the circles and links can be added later with a pencil on the printout (see Figure 2-3). Computers with even the simplest of word processing programs provide the ability to move ideas about, testing their grouping, trying out the relationships. Once ideas have been generated, a central idea can be identified and marked to be copied to the top of the screen (for a tree), or moved to the middle of the screen (for a web), or moved to a section of the screen (for clustering or diagraming). Other ideas can be arranged or linked accordingly. The actual drawing of the web or cluster is not as important as the activity of grouping and linking, which acts as a stimulus for further thought and better writing.

Devil's Advocate

Before lawyers enter a courtroom, they have a sense of what their opponent's arguments will be. They are prepared to counter those arguments with logic and legal precedence. Good lawyers prepare the case for the other side—their opponent—to know what they are up against, a device known as playing the devil's advocate. Writers, especially those using a computer, can take advantage of this technique. To do this, a writer creates two sides to the computer screen, by making windows or creating columns, each of which is now standard with most word processing programs. The split screen can be divided horizontally or vertically. Even elementary or older programs can accomplish this by setting the margins for the page from 10 to 35 and 40 to 65. The two sides can be labeled *our case* and *their case*. As ideas are added to the two cases, they can be rearranged to correspond by using the copy/move sequence.

For example, a student writing a paper dealing with economics might wish to offer feasible solutions to the growing problem of inflation. Instead of simply considering the traditional methods of fighting inflation, the student might gain useful insights by playing the devil's advocate. The student could ask what economic activities need to be continued although they contribute to inflation and what impact would the traditional inflation-fighting tactics have upon these important considerations. By looking at the devil's case, writers can strengthen their own positions. Writers can eventually use both sides of the argument by constructing rhetorical phrases, such as "some might believe . . . , but. . . ."

Even students who are unsure which side they wish to support can use this strategy. The computer will create a space for pro and con. On the pro side of the screen, the writer enters points in favor of that particular side of the issue. On the con side, the writer tries to offer the counter arguments, lining the cursor up across from the corresponding "pro" argument. When finished, the writer simply chooses a side to defend, ordinarily the side with the most unanswered arguments. This strategy can be taught for assignments dealing with comparison (how two or more things are alike) and contrast (how two or more things are different from each other).

Rhetorical Prompts

In the early 1980s, composition teachers saw the possibility of creating computer programs to aid writers, ones that would mimic the helpful probes and prods of a sympathetic writing teacher (LeBlanc 1993). My computer program, QUEST, for example, would ask a variety of questions, inserting the topic and previous answers in slots left blank in the programming. For example, on the screen QUEST would ask:

Chapter Two Helping Students Generate Written Text

OKAY, **Jason** [*inserting the student's name*]
WHAT WAS **gun control** LIKE IN THE PAST? WHAT WILL IT BE LIKE IN THE FUTURE? [*inserting the student's topic*]
TYPE YOUR RESPONSE HERE —>

The problems became obvious. Sometimes the topic didn't fit in the sentence:

OKAY, **Jason**
WHAT WAS **Civil War** LIKE IN THE PAST? WHAT WILL IT BE LIKE IN THE FUTURE?
TYPE YOUR RESPONSE HERE —>

Sometimes the topic wasn't worded properly for the computer:

OKAY, **Jason**
WHAT WAS **the way my parents don't listen to me** LIKE IN THE PAST? WHAT WILL IT BE LIKE IN THE FUTURE?
TYPE YOUR RESPONSE HERE —>

The computer responded to the topic as only a variable string of words to be assigned places in sentences, never as a meaningful phrase. No matter how much work was done to make these programs more sophisticated and to create intelligent tutors, the computer, without human understanding, could not simulate human response.

Others tried to solve the problem by changing the prompts to requests for students to supply parts of speech. One program, using prompts for slot-and-fill poetry, CINQ2, was written by Joseph Hackett (1991), a teacher at the Sir Winston Churchill High School in St. Laurent, Quebec, Canada. The program was designed to generate a cinquain, a five-line poem, by prompting students with a series of requests: "give me a noun; give me two adjectives; give me three verbs with *-ing* endings; give me an action verb in a phrase; and finally, give me a noun that substitutes for the first noun." The computer would then assemble each answer into a five-line poem (and add, "Great job" for positive reinforcement). The poem might be:

Cows.
serene, congenial.
mooing, chewing, staring.
masticate with intensity.
Bovines.

This may be fun, but it's not real poetry. It's formula. This may be a poetry exercise, but it's as much poetry as a processed cheese product is cheese. Real writing is meaningful and authentic; this is something else. Whatever else happens, there is little transfer of writing strategy to be used outside the confines of the poetry writing program.

Guidance Files

While working on the problem of trying to create a computer program that would respond meaningfully to text, Dawn and Ray Rodrigues (1986) found a less sophisticated way to approach the problem. Rather than writing programming code, which would make the computer run automatically once the student began a program, Dawn and Ray Rodrigues suggested using word processing files to give short lessons on writing, lessons that were interactive in the sense that students entered information in appropriate places within the files. These guidance files, which they called lesson files, dealt with separate rhetorical activities. For example, one guidance file might be named FIVE-W's. A student who retrieved that file would receive a lesson, an explanation of the five w's—who, what, where, when, and why—and could interact by answering the five w's concerning a topic of their own choosing. When the student finished and saved the file on their disk, the student had both the questions and the answers, any or all of which could be copied to another file for drafting.

Numerous examples of lesson files can be found in Dawn and Ray Rodrigues' *Teaching Writing with a Word Processor, Grades 7–13* (1986), but any teacher can create these customized guidance files. One of my favorite guidance files that students of all

Chapter Two Helping Students Generate Written Text

ages seem to enjoy, including graduate students, is called PIRATE. It is based on a guidance file created in my graduate workshop by Laurie Morrison, a teacher in the New Wilmington school district in Pennsylvania, who designed PIRATE to help her students work on character development.

****
               PIRATE   Screen 1
****

When a writer thinks of the characters that will be a part of a story, the writer creates a mental picture of that character. The writer then decides what personality traits that character will have. For example, will the character be friendly? sensitive? aggressive? successful? selfish?

As a writer, you have the power to develop your own characters, letting the reader know what type of person your character really is and how your character acts.

In this lesson you will answer questions about your character and write about him or her, using that information. This is what we call a character sketch. You may press the page up key to review your answers at any time.

****
               PIRATE   Screen 2
****

After you have read the instructions, close your eyes and imagine a pirate. Look closely at your pirate and notice all of the details that may give you clues about the type of person he is and how he may act (most pirates were men, but feel free to create a female pirate, if you wish). Now close your eyes and imagine your pirate. After you have pictured him, proceed to the next frame.

****
               PIRATE   Screen 3
****

Now answer the following questions about your pirate in as

much detail as you can. Type in your answer next to each question.

a. What is your pirate's name?
b. Why did he decide to become a pirate?
c. How does your pirate talk? Does he have an accent?
d. How does he laugh? Use comparison.
e. How does he walk?
f. Are there any unique features about his appearance?
g. Visualize your pirate one more time and add any other important facts that would describe him.

```
****************************************************************
                PIRATE              Screen 4
****************************************************************
```

Now that you have decided the appearance of your character, concentrate on how the character feels by answering the following questions as completely as you can.

a. What would make your pirate happy?
b. What would make your pirate sad?
c. What would make your pirate frustrated?
d. What would confuse your pirate?

Now you have suggested the personality of your character. By answering those questions, you have decided what type of individual he is and what is important to him. Check to see if there is anything else you would like to add.

```
****************************************************************
                PIRATE              Screen 5
****************************************************************
```

Place your pirate in the following situations and figure out how he would react in each. Write a description of his actions after each. How would your pirate react:

a. if he saw a treasure ship?
b. if someone gave him a gift?

c. to a child who was crying?
d. if he was hurt?
e. if he saw a beggar?
f. when meeting an old friend?

By answering these questions you have decided how your character interacts with other people and how he acts in different situations. Review your answers and see if there are any more details you could add.

****
                    PIRATE   Screen 6
****

A. *Return to screen 3* and, using the copy/move sequence and the insert/delete functions, write a paragraph describing your pirate, using your previous answers to the questions.
B. *Return to screen 4* and write a paragraph describing your pirate's personality by using your previous answers.
C. *Return to screen 5* and write a paragraph describing how your pirate reacts in different situations. Use your previous answers.

****
                    PIRATE   Screen 7
****

Well done! You have just completed the rough draft for your character sketch. Review each paragraph, adding information if needed and removing nonessential details. You might also check your paragraphs for spelling and punctuation errors. When you are satisfied with each paragraph, save your character sketch file and print out a hard copy. Once completed, exit the word processing program.

****
                    PIRATE   The End
****

Completing guidance files such as PIRATE sparks ideas for variations of the character sketch. Some teachers create guidance files to generate characters in creative writing assignments and others use them to analyze characters in a class reading. Although authors of novels go to great lengths to describe their characters, each reader gets to know each character a little differently. The guidance file might be a suitable way to ask readers to place the character in a new situation. For example, a teacher might ask students reading *The Outsiders* how Pony Boy would react if he:

a. saw a homeless person?
b. was sent flowers?
c. won the state lottery?
d. woke up with a zit?

Students could react to each other's answers to the prompts, deciding as a class who responded to the situation the way the character would and who substituted their own reactions.

Collaborative Prewriting

Students can sometimes use the ideas their classmates generate to suggest ideas of their own. Collaborative prewriting can be done with two students taking turns at one computer, two students carrying on an exchange over a network (see Chapter 4 for further discussion of networks), or two students exchanging keyboards (a variation of Stephen Marcus' invisible writing, where the text that a student types appears on the other student's screen because of the crossed keyboards (Marcus 1991; Derrick 1986)).

For example, a collaborative prewriting activity might have students work together on separate topics. One student might type:

> The mass media—TV news, news magazine shows, talk shows, the "hard copy" entertainment news—love scandals. The political and religious scandals that are the greatest audience generators are responsible for the lack of faith or trust in

our two greatest institutions—the democratic government and the church.

The second student would be instructed to think about what had been written and what the situation described reminds him or her of. The student would then write on his/her computer:

> This reminds me of when brothers and sisters tell on each other, reporting the least infraction, hoping to win favor with their parents. But it usually backfires because the parents don't like the "squealing" kid any better; they lose faith in both kids, the informer and the guilty one.

Both students could try to react by looking for a commonality in the two situations. The first student might write:

> Everyone loses when they try to climb over each other.

The other might come up with:

> Knowledge (reporting) is not always as welcome as we thought.

The collaborators could trade observations back and forth, amplifying their comments and synthesizing their observations about what the other has written until they have an understanding that they would not have otherwise had. At this point they are free to finish their writing using any or all of the collaborative prewriting ideas they coauthored.

Finding Out More

Our romantic notion of writing tells us that if students will just turn within and examine what they already know about subjects, they will be able to write. Sometimes the knowledge is not contained within, and no matter how much meditation or contemplation is done, the knowledge will not come. That's when we'd send our students to the library. Today the computer can make that trip unnecessary, thanks to CD-ROM technology.

The CD-ROM disk player works like another drive in the computer, allowing students to load what amounts to a superdisk, one big enough to hold an encyclopedia's worth of information. In fact, these laser disks (which look exactly like music compact discs) typically will hold all of an encyclopedia's volumes or a bookshelf of almanac materials. Jamie Sue Crouse, a twelfth grader at Hempfield Area High School in Pennsylvania, says, "If I find I know very little about the subject, I . . . open up the *Grolier's Encyclopedia* [on CD-ROM], research my subject, and then I return to my brainstorming list." A classmate, Carolyn Baker, concurs, "If, in the process of writing . . . I need to check a fact, I merely access the encyclopedia that I have on CD-ROM, check my facts, and return quickly to my paper." In fact, Carolyn says if she reads something that is particularly relevant, she can highlight it and transfer the copy as a direct quote in her paper.

An eleventh grader at Hempfield, Diane Persin, says that, when using an electronic encyclopedia with a sound card in her computer, "I can not only read John F. Kennedy's famous inaugural address, but listen to it as I do research." Heather Lambing, another Hempfield student, recommends her *Microsoft Bookshelf* CD-ROM because it contains seven sets of books—each set containing as many as thirty volumes—on one compact disc: an atlas, a dictionary, an almanac, two books of quotations, and two thesauri. "Each reference book . . . provides a different outlook on the topic" being researched, Heather says.

The danger exists that writers fall into unrestricted or unregulated borrowing from CD-ROMs. It's one thing to read in order to gain information to help generate material for a written composition. It's another thing to simply import material. My first experience with CD-ROMs involved a student turning in a seven-page paper for an assignment that asked for one to two pages on a topic of personal interest. Ron's interest was gambling, and he produced what amounted to a "history of gambling." He had authored it only in the sense that he used his CD-ROM to locate the encyclopedia entry on gambling and downloaded the information to his paper. He had no sense that it was plagiarism or bad research; he was quite proud of the paper. More than ever before, teachers will be required to demonstrate that generating material for a writing assignment involves digesting material from other sources, using summarizing and paraphrasing skills. This is much easier to do when students have choice of topic and are interested in making the knowledge theirs. Rather than failing Ron for plagiarism, I asked him to read the information he had downloaded and to say it in his own words without exceeding the two-page limit. Too often students get the impression that changing a few words or rearranging sentences does the trick. Ron found that doing research meant synthesizing information from a variety of sources (including his personal observations and interviews).

Once material has been written, the computer can help writers revise, edit, and proofread their work, using the features available on most word processing programs, and collaborate with their teachers and others, conferencing in the classroom, over a network, and on the Internet.

Chapter Three

Helping Students Revise Written Text

One of the temptations of writing with computers is that students equate drafting with writing. The magic of word processing has made students focus on drafting text, ignoring the importance of prewriting and revision. The words flow, the text grows, and teachers are reading student texts that are lengthy, neatly printed, and mechanically correct (thanks to spell checkers). And yet, something is not quite right. Students are writing more and have a better attitude toward writing, but the writing isn't better. The computer hasn't, after all, seemed to create texts that are substantively better than what the students produced in the past, using pen and paper. How can this be? Perhaps it is because computers have been used as production tools, much the way pens and typewriters were used. We need to use the computer to support the whole writing process. We need to use the computer as an instructional tool rather than just a production tool.

Teaching revision assumes that writers have generated ideas, have sufficient amounts of text to work with, and understand revision is not the same as editing. The computer has the power to change writers' conception of revision. Yet simply having students work with computers will not automatically make them better revisers, and computers and word processing cannot, in themselves, teach revision. The very ease of generating text with a computer causes a writer's attention to be directed to making the final version conform to standard edited English (spelling, usage, grammar, punctuation). Teachers must facilitate revision by modeling, demonstrating, suggesting, and encouraging revision.

Teachers need strategies for revision that help students reflect on their writing as it takes shape and that allow the computer to do what is impossible or unlikely to be done with handwritten-text revision. And the beauty of teaching revision with the computer, as any writer will attest, is that after every change, the alteration is undetectable. Revision with word processing makes every draft look like an original, alleviating some of the aggravation of revision, the rewriting headache—copying over a revised text, the cosmetics of revision.

Revision means to envision another version; re-vision: to imagine what is not—to imagine the better text. Revision means being able to recast sentences, alter diction, and rethink organization. Tom Reigstad and Don McAndrew (1984) refer to these considerations as Higher-Order Concerns (HOCs), those pertaining to focus, voice, organization, and development. If students are directed to reconsider these concerns, computers offer students a chance to see a need for revision in their own writing through the electronic manipulation of their text files. This is not to say that word processing makes revision simple or easy. Substantive revision is tedious and hard work.

Students ask what they have to do to make their writing better. Some experts say students "need to learn to look at their writing though the reader's eye, noticing gaps in the information, precarious inductive leaps, and missing links" (Guth 1988), but it may not be that easy. To know how to do those things requires vision. When my daughter was in tenth grade I asked her how she made her papers better. Laura told me that when she gets a chance to work on a paper again, she fixes the words that jump out at her. She adds sentences and changes a few words (if she thinks of better ones). She remembered adding a sentence to the end of her last paper. I asked one of her classmates the same question when Laura wasn't around. She said that she waits for the teacher to tell her where to "add some details." If the teacher doesn't actually tell her, or isn't available, then she goes to someone "who is really smart" and has that person read it. Otherwise, she doesn't know what to do.

As ineffective as these revision strategies seem, writers become fixated with the way they approach revision—good or bad. Mike Rose (1980) referred to this dilemma as writers having rigid rules and inflexible strategies; writers revise in a particular way because that's the way they've always done it. Students develop idiosyncratic strategies for revising their papers: they make it longer, adding more to the end of the text; they substitute words; they correct punctuation, grammar, and spelling. To learn more substantive revision, however, they must see a need for revision and be open to suggestions for possibilities. These conditions are more likely to occur if the students are writing about topics of their own choosing to an audience of real readers, rather than a topic assigned by and read by their teacher. Revision becomes important because of the investment writers make.

The following strategies are offered as devices to use in classrooms as writers learn to revise with a "reader's eye." I am not suggesting that these are strategies that experienced writers use; however, less experienced writers may find the techniques helpful in developing more productive revision strategies as they experiment and learn to "re-see" their writing. These strategies help less experienced writers move away from their drafts to look at them from different perspectives, a talent that takes time and practice to develop. Different strategies will appeal to different writers, and as with all the strategies suggested in this book, each writer will find some approaches work better than others.

Outlining

At some point, everyone has been taught to create an outline, a skeleton of their plan, organized according to the relative importance of ideas—a thesis subdivided according to major ideas, then further subdivided according to points to be made under each major idea, and that in turn divided into subpoints. A brainstormed list, such as one suggested in the previous chapter, provides somewhat the same skeletal plan without the indication of levels of importance.

Outlines seem to make the act of writing logical and sequential. Perhaps that is why outlines are sometimes required for longer pieces of writing, such as term papers or other projects requiring organized plans.

For years, I believed I was the only one who subverted the purpose of completing an outline by writing it *after* I had finished my research paper. I would read over my draft, looking for major categories of ideas. I would write these down in order, labeling them with Roman numerals—I, II, III. Once I found the major categories, I would read the paper looking for subheadings I could use, often any topic discussed for a paragraph or two. These I would label with capital letters—A, B, C. If really pressed, I would find a detail or two that I could include under each letter, labeling those with the lowercase Roman numerals—i, ii, iii. Finding the major ideas was so much easier after I had written them.

In doing my "post-facto" outline, I noticed that I could spot places where my thoughts did not really flow from one to the next. This turned out to be a test for coherence. With an outline of what I had written—a skeleton—I could test each heading as the means of getting to the next heading, which then became the means to the following heading. In this fashion, each heading advanced toward establishing the conclusion, the final heading. If I found that, as a reader, I could not move logically from one heading to the next, then I knew I needed to write more, teasing out the argument, explanation, or exposition.

The longer a piece of writing becomes, the more difficult it is to check how well a piece of writing holds together. A post-facto outline can become a useful revision strategy. And if writers are working on a computer, a variation of my post-facto outline can be produced quickly to check coherence.

After students have written drafts, teachers can direct them to save the original and create a copy by renaming the file with an .OUT file extension (e.g., the file PAPER#1.DOC would be renamed PAPER#1.OUT). Because the writer's draft is safely stored under the original name, the writer can create an outline form by identifying the sentence within each paragraph containing the paragraph's major idea. Once the sentence has been marked, the writer reduces the paragraph by stripping everything else from each paragraph, using the block/delete function. For my students who have difficulty with the "major idea" concept, I direct them to work backward, deleting sentences in the paragraph until they find the one sentence that absolutely cannot be sacrificed.

Wholesale deletion of text will probably cause anxiety the first time writers try the strategy because it means erasing everything but one sentence in a paragraph. Teachers need to be aware of that anxiety and reassure the students by showing that the original draft is safely saved on their disk. When writers repeat the reducing sequence for each paragraph, all the original paragraphs will be represented by an equal number of sentences.

Moreover, teachers who recommend that their writers use a thesis sentence can have students examine their post-facto sentence outlines to find one sentence that seems to express what the writer intends to show with the paper as a whole. Writers can then duplicate the sentence identified as the most important and copy it to the top of the writer's post-facto outline to act as the thesis statement. The sentences that remain beneath the thesis sentence can be sequenced, if so desired, by capital and lowercase letters and Roman and Arabic numbers.

Teachers can direct their students to get a printout of each outline and then retrieve their original files. When the writers save and store the outline file and return the original file to the screen, teachers might take the opportunity to remind them about the difference between the two documents. For example, I renamed my PAPER#1.DOC file as PAPER#1.OUT for the outline, an example of how the three-letter extension in the name can prevent a writer from losing track of the files (DOC is the original document; OUT is the outline version of it).

Writers should have a printout of the outline placed next to them while revising the draft. This way, each writer can examine and evaluate the outline for coherence by asking, does idea #2 (Roman numeral II) lead into idea #3 (Roman numeral III)? Does another idea need to be discussed (idea #2a) to make the connection, or does each flow into the next idea? If the writer feels the need for more explanation, he or she can write more or leave a brief note to indicate what might be written later. The analysis of coherence continues until the writer is satisfied.

Windowing

Most word processing programs enable writers to divide the computer screen into two windows, as mentioned in the previous chapter. The windowing feature can help revision. After executing the window sequence, a writer can enter either window with the directional arrow keys and move through the text, scrolling with the arrow keys or the page up/page down keys, or load a different file into one of the windows, recalling the outline file, PAPER#1.OUT, for example. While active in the window, the writer can do any of the standard word processing activities: write or revise text, save it, print it, and exit from it.

Windowing is a valuable strategy to use any time a writer wants to be able to compare documents or look at two parts of a text at the same time, page eight and page two, for example. Windowing allows a writer to compare two versions of the same assignment, such as one written by a classmate and one by the student. This feature also allows a writer to use a successful earlier assignment as a model for a current paper being worked on.

The writer has the potential to jump to the other window at any time, if so desired. Once there, the writer can perform the same actions as before, while the previously active window stays fixed. For example, the writer could load the brainstormed list or the post-facto outline into the top window and then hop to the bottom window to revise the original draft according to the insights gained from examining the list or outline. The windows ensure that the writer always has the plan in view. Some word processing programs let the writer use a small onscreen note pad to jot down ideas. These small windows are sometimes called "note pad" or "comment" features.

Once the draft has been compared with the original outline, and text has been added, adjusted, or deleted, writers can return the screen to one whole file by closing the window displaying the other file.

Sentence Separation

Looking at only one part of a puzzle at a time can help writers revise. A strategy for revision developed by Wendy Paterson (1988) of Buffalo State College is relatively simple: teachers direct their students to go back to the beginning of their draft and insert blank lines between each sentence in the text by pressing the enter key twice after each period. This separates each sentence of the writer's draft from the others, allowing writers to look at each sentence on its own, reading it by itself, without the distraction of the rest of the words around it. As always, writers should save the original file and create a second copy by renaming it with a .SEN extension (e.g., the file PAPER#1.DOC would be renamed PAPER#1.SEN).

The sentence separation strategy allows writers to examine pairs of sentences to see if another sentence needs to come between the pair to help the progression of ideas. A writer who wants to elaborate need only hit the return key and write more or leave a brief note to indicate what might be written later. The writing will expand like an accordion, avoiding once more the tedious "copy-over" aspect of revision. Likewise the separation of the sentences can help writers notice where a sentence doesn't add anything to the essay, allowing them to simply delete any superfluous sentences or use sentence-combining skills to consolidate the sentences.

When the writers have finished looking at their sentences in isolation, they have the choice of simply pressing the delete key twice after every period to put the sentences back in place or returning to their original undisturbed file.

Cumulative Sentences

Students are often told to revise by developing their ideas, adding more details, or being more specific. The sentence separation strategy offers teachers a chance to give students a concrete revision strategy, the creation of cumulative sentences, teaching students to add right-branch modifiers to sentences, elaborating on the basic premise, explaining a term, or completing a thought the way this sentence does. This strategy is based on Francis Christensen's (1978) generative rhetoric, which is developing, adding, and specifying by writing noun phrases, verb phrases, and absolutes. For example, a student could be directed to return to any sentence in their essay, one such as this:

Dave stood patiently at the corner.

The student would then be instructed to add a noun phrase to describe any noun in the sentence, in this case, Dave or the corner. Here are two noun phrases:

Dave, *a recent graduate of Robert's School of Mixology,* stood patiently at the corner, *a busy spot for the late hour of 3:00 A.M.*

The student could add a verb phrase to describe the action in the sentence, in this case, standing at the corner:

Dave stood patiently at the corner, *waiting for the last bus.*

Or the student could add an absolute phrase, a reduced sentence:

Dave, *a man tired from his first day at work,* stood patiently at the corner.

A student might even take risks and use all the ideas generated in the revision activity:

> Dave, a recent graduate of Robert's School of Mixology, a man tired from his first day at work, stood patiently at the corner, a busy spot for the late hour of 3:00 A.M., waiting for the last bus.

Sentence-combining techniques can encourage the student to try different arrangements and variations:

> Waiting for the last bus and tired from his first day at work, Dave, a recent graduate of Robert's School of Mixology, stood patiently at the corner, a busy spot for the late hour of 3:00 A.M.

Compare this sentence with the original: *Dave stood patiently at the corner.* Students who have been shown Christensen's principle may return to any point in the text to add information, generating more ideas that, in turn, spark more thoughts. This type of strategy works best with sentences from the students' own writing rather than sentence-combining exercises on disk. The strategy, to be effective, must help writers re-envision their own drafts.

Word processing encourages cumulative sentence revision because it moves the text over to make room for the new modifiers, and with "word wrap" and "paragraph reformatting" features, the revised text is undetectable from the original. Because the computer adjusts everything so that the text looks untouched, its modified form has what Helen Schwartz (1986) calls "visual credibility." The same strategy using pen and paper for this activity leaves a trail of strike-overs, arrows, and crossouts. The advantages are obvious.

The Power of Paragraphs

Some writers are puzzled about when to begin a new paragraph. Advice from handbooks tells writers to begin a new paragraph when a new idea is begun. Experts who study readability tell writers the average length of paragraphs is approximately ninety-five words, leaving writers to infer that a new paragraph might begin every 100 words or so. My advice to writers is the same as I give them for starting a new sentence: begin a new one when you've finished with the previous one. After all, the real problem of when to start a new paragraph is knowing when the previous one is finished. Some writers do not know when they are finished, so they just keep writing the same paragraph.

My nephew, Ken, a junior at Penfield High School in Rochester, New York, finds paragraphing distracting to him as a writer. He let me read a two and a half–page, single-spaced essay he wrote about *The Crucible*. It was one paragraph. Ken let me read his nine-page historical fiction narrating the life of a first generation American during the Civil War. Again, no paragraphs. Ken is not a novice writer; he composes on the computer and he regularly wins awards for his writing. He simply finds paragraphing unnecessary. To Ken, paragraphing, double-spacing, and even spell checking, are editing considerations, tasks best left until later, tasks often forgotten about. I admit that worrying about when to begin and end paragraphs can be a distraction while generating material, but paragraphing can be a generative process, one helpful for revision.

A draft finished as one long paragraph, even a nine-page paragraph, or finished as numerous long paragraphs, can be restructured as several shorter paragraphs. Ironically, paragraphing might best be taught as a revision activity, since a writer cannot decide to restructure long paragraphs until after they have been written. With typed or handwritten drafts, decisions to make long paragraphs into shorter ones mean rewriting the entire paper, a task most hope to avoid. But when writing with a computer, it's easily done.

With a completed draft, writers begin reading until they reach a section that feels like a new aspect of the paper, a place where the subject begins to change or the words give that "and another thing . . ." feeling. A new paragraph may be about to begin, but there's no way to know for sure without trying it out. I showed Ken how the computer would allow him to try out various places to begin paragraphs. At the beginning of the suspected paragraph, Ken simply pressed the enter key. This moved the text after the cursor to the next line, where the tab key or the spacebar could indent the text to form a new paragraph.

As a writer, Ken knew he wasn't committed to the paragraph just because he created it. As a writer using a computer, he could look back at the paragraph to see how it read, and if he liked it, he would continue the paragraph creation. However, if he felt the new paragraph wasn't quite right, the original paragraph could be restored by moving the cursor to the concluding period and pressing the delete key until the paragraph was rejoined. Ken continued in this fashion, splitting paragraphs and evaluating, until he finished the document.

I convinced Ken to paragraph with the argument that it was a courtesy to his readers—the white space made his paper easier to read. But Ken quickly realized that once he had split his extended paragraphs, he could take advantage of another revision strategy, adding information and detail to a draft at any point—within a draft, within a paragraph, even within a sentence.

My students, like many others, when writing by hand tend to add to the *end* of their drafts (a strategy confirmed as popular by Colette Dauite's 1986 research with young writers), because adding details anywhere other than the end would mean copying the whole paper over. When writing with a computer, however, my students can add details anywhere in their papers while retaining "visual credibility."

Conclusions for Introductions

If writers are terrified of blank pages, it's no wonder introductory paragraphs are often embarrassing, clunky, strained, and generally formulaic. My friend Tom and I developed our own formula for writing papers that we used from high school to college. We would begin any and every paper this way: "To say that [*insert a standard interpretation here*] is to ignore the importance of [*insert our insight here*]." So an English literature paper might begin:

> To say that Hamlet is paralyzed by indecision is to ignore the importance of Hamlet's unsuccessful attempts to assert his self-esteem before various members of and visitors to the court.

A philosophy paper might begin:

> To say that the narrator in Camus' *The Stranger* embodies twentieth century existentialism is to ignore the significance of Camus' rejection of Kant's categorical imperative.

Sometimes even the music reviews we wrote for the student newspaper would contain the same formula:

> It goes without saying that "Sunshine of Your Love" establishes Cream's status as the greatest power trio in rock 'n' roll, but we must not ignore the contribution of the fourth member of the "trio," their producer, the person who truly shapes the sound we applaud.

My students often come to my classes with less prosaic standard openings: "One of the most controversial issues today is [*insert issue here: handgun control, abortion, censorship, the ecology movement*]." Some write more functional introductions: "This paper will discuss the three causes of [*insert issue here*]." These beginnings are not wrong, but I suggest to my students that they continue to use these formulas as a way to begin writing, but then use the *conclusions for introductions* strategy.

I explain the conclusions for introductions strategy this way: if writing is a mode of learning, then the conclusion, not the introduction, is where writers find what they wanted to say. Writers, when they begin, are uncertain what their point is going to be. Donald Murray (1984) says he is always surprised by his writing; in writing, he says, he discovers what he thinks. In the act of writing the conclusion, writers are forced to summarize what they've discovered, to make some closing remarks, to have a big finish. Writers use the knowledge they've gained in the process of writing the entire paper to write the conclusion.

Yet, if writers make their readers struggle through the same discovery process, they are writing a mystery—nothing is clear until the end. Readers usually need this information much earlier, perhaps at the beginning. After all, when writers are ready to conclude their work, they have just completed the discovery of that which their readers need to know at the beginning of the piece of writing. I suggest that writers do their readers a favor by moving their conclusion to the beginning, substituting it for the formulaic introduction. This activity teaches a strategy for revision that turns writer-based prose into reader-based prose (Flower 1979).

Once again, this change can be done much more easily if using word processing. Direct students to use the copy/move sequence to mark the text of the conclusion. After the concluding paragraph is blocked, it can be moved using the appropriate function key to the beginning, and it will then appear as the new introduction ahead of what was formerly the introduction, which can then be deleted the way scaffolding is removed, or it can be moved and rewritten.

Once the "what was formerly the introduction" is replaced with the conclusion, the writer will be missing a conclusion. If the writer is in a hurry, the old introduction could always be used as the new conclusion. Readers are more tolerant of a formulaic ending if the rest of the paper has been engaging. But ideally it is better to write another ending. Instead of simply writing a summary of what was said, I suggest trying a quotation or writing an anecdote to wrap it all up. My students are soon convinced that writing an ending is a great deal easier than writing a beginning; that is, easier when writing with a computer.

Collaborative Revision

An editor, a teacher, or another writer can often respond to a piece of writing in ways that an author can't. Text that has been written in a certain way tends to obstruct seeing alternatives. An author becomes so familiar with the original approach that it is difficult to see ways to reorganize the writing. It is equally difficult to see where advance organizers might be necessary, where elaboration is called for, where an opinion or thesis needs to be rethought, and where coherence, clarity, and logic need to be strengthened.

Taking a fresh look at the writing by moving text and modifying constructions can help encourage revision. Although writers can try out various arrangements of their essays, I recommend strategies that ask students to work in pairs for collaborative revision, taking turns as writer and reader for each other.

The first activity has the author, after having saved the original file, scramble the order of the paragraphs in a writing, using the copy/move function of the word processing program, and asking a second student to reassemble the paragraphs using the same function. The writer compares the newly arranged writing with the original, noting insights from the ways a reader made sense of text.

A second activity has the author, once again saving the original file, remove the paragraph indentations so the writing reads as one continuous text. A second student then tries to insert the paragraph breaks. The original writer may even give the reader a clue as to how many paragraphs to make. The results will be informative, regardless of whether the two agree on where the breaks should come. (Of course, this activity should be done with either a different pair of writers or with a writing assignment different from the one used previously.)

A third collaborative activity uses the sentence separation technique to isolate and then scramble the order of the sentences (using the copy/move feature). The author asks a classmate to try to re-order the sentences. A reader may see the sentences in a different way. Once again, the results will be informative, whatever the outcome.

A fourth activity is a variation of the deleting operation of the post-facto outlining strategy. Working in pairs, students are asked to examine a portion of their partner's text—a page, a paragraph, a section with a heading—and to delete a superfluous sentence (functionally defined as one the reader feels the text could exist without). The students can advance to the next section of the texts and repeat the deletion of superfluous sentences until the entire text has been examined. If combined with the sentence separation exercise, the pairs can also suggest to each other where another sentence or two needs to be written to help the forward progression of the ideas.

The trimming and elaboration suggestions, as with all the collaborative activities, should be performed on a duplicate copy of the text, leaving the writer free to endorse or adopt the suggestions they judge as helpful. Whether they agree with the classmate's suggestions is less important than the reflective stance that these exercises cause writers to take when a reader suggests that they delete or add sentences to their completed work.

To revise is to see another version, a clearer text. Revision means to imagine what is not, to recast sentences, alter diction, and rethink organization. Revision means taking a fresh look; the combination of the technology of the computer and the strategies for moving words, sentences, and paragraphs, and adding and deleting text helps writers see global revision in action.

Chapter Four

Helping Students Collaborate and Conference

Teachers of writing have two major tasks: to get students to write about topics the students care about and to provide responses to their writings in a timely fashion, ideally during the process. Teachers can use computers to generate a series of drafts for readers—the teacher and/or classmates—and to accommodate the exchange of responses from readers during writing conferences, thereby providing feedback while writings are still in progress. Many teachers value having their students write to each other during the drafting, revising, and editing of papers. Teachers also value having a real audience for writing, one including students and adults outside the classroom. Writers, sharing similar interests or assignments, can offer their reactions to each other's writings, providing a stimulus to further writing.

I have had students exchange papers in progress with students in another section of English composition and with students in other subjects (psychology, history). My wife, Kathleen, is having her preservice teachers write to students at an elementary school in an impoverished urban area. Our daughter Laura is having her junior high class of emotional-support students write to a class of first grade students in another state.

Teachers have been doing the paper exchange long before there were computers, but the obvious problem with these exchanges is the time they take. When the two groups are in the same building, the exchange can be accomplished within days, but as the distance increases, so does the time necessary to complete a cycle. Teachers need an exchange method that approximates the immediacy of the phone system rather than the postal system; in short, teachers need what computers can provide.

E-mail Correspondence

Jane Cowden (1996), a teacher at Big Spring High School, conducts a variation on the paper exchange using e-mail correspondence. Jane's Cross-Grade Letter Writing Project has elementary, high school, and university students writing to each other in groups of three, one from each grade level. In her directions to the university participants, Jane writes, "Primarily, you will be discussing the topic of the writing: sharing your personal writing experiences, offering suggestions on how to solve writing problems, discussing some of your own writing concerns, and if you wish, sharing some pieces of writing."

The entire exchange is conducted with the computer. Letters are written to Jane's e-mail address with the intended student's name indicated. Jane forwards the letter to the recipient, who then writes a reply, routing it through Jane's mailbox. If the students had their own e-mail addresses, the letter writing could be done directly, but Jane feels more comfortable monitoring the "language and the content of the letters since the little kids will be reading not only the letters addressed to them but also the ones [written] to the high school student." This indirect delivery arrangement is not the best setup, but in this age of concern, principals and parents are less worried knowing an adult is supervising the project.

I entered into e-mail conversations with some of Jane's students this year. One tenth grader, Rebecca Chamberlin, wrote, "This year I have begun writing poetry and I have been playing with the format a lot. I have discovered that the font used has a great influence on the interpretation of the poetry. For example, I have only one font (that is horrendous) on my computer. I formatted [a poem] any way on "the dinosaur" [what she calls her ancient computer at home] and looked [at it]. I then retyped it using a better font on a more current computer [at school] and it was much more successful. I will send you some of my poetry if you wish . . ."

I e-mailed back that same day, suggesting to Rebecca that she try using the enter key and the spacebar to experiment with the spatial design of poetry. I explained that with typographic changes (changing appearance, letter spacing, pitch, and typeface) and spatial arrangement, the computer would give her a chance to try "what if" arrangements with the words she has written.

The next morning there was a message from Rebecca: "I was surprised to get [your reply] so quickly." She continued to say that she would send me her poetry later because she had a "hectic week coming up" and "a portfolio due in this class this week." This brief exchange illustrates how comfortable Rebecca felt in an electronic conversation and how she was willing to engage in writing when the topic was of her own choosing.

Conferencing

Every writer has had the experience of having someone else read what has been written and getting the response, "Oh, I thought you meant . . ." or "I took this to mean . . ." Readers get lost in the text, make alternative constructions, modify those meanings, and in the end, arrive at a sense of what it all means. Because texts have readers, what any given text says is not exactly what the author intended, and each reader takes an active part in the construction of meaning. Writers who are genuinely interested in how their writing will be received are happy to have reader feedback.

When reading another's draft on paper, readers take physical possession of the paper, picking it up, holding it in their hands, actually taking the copy away from the author. The effect is not just physical; the reader has taken possession, psychological ownership. Sometimes a reader will even take out a pen to comment on the paper, defacing it in a sense. Teachers can become

Chapter Four Helping Students Collaborate and Conference

desensitized to the effect marking up a paper has, regarding it as simply helping. Students may allow, even ask, teachers to mark up their papers, but they are often less gracious about having others do it and uncomfortable when asked to write comments on another's work.

Taking physical possession of a paper is unnecessary when reading another's text on a computer screen; the computer's presentation of the text causes a subtle difference in ownership: even while reading text on a screen, the writing belongs to the writer. During conferencing, a reader can comfortably sit side by side with the author at the computer—reading, negotiating meaning, and commenting on the text. The reader is *supporting the writer* rather than *fixing the writing*; if changes are made, the writer makes them.

Comments in the Text

Computer collaboration can be a natural revision strategy: writers talk to each other, reading and commenting on the work of their peers while receiving comments about their own work that they will need when revising. A number of software programs facilitate collaboration by allowing readers to place editorial comments inside a writer's text without altering the original document. Most programs are able to divide the screen into separate windows, one displaying the original text, the other providing space for collaborative response. Some programs allow writers to either exchange texts or edit the same document simultaneously without seeing each other's suggestions. Some will merge group comments into a single annotated text while retaining each reader's individual comments for later review (see Appendix B).

But purchasing special software is not necessary, as long as readers understand how to use some elementary word processing features. If readers simply duplicate the file by renaming it, they can write comments within the text without altering the original document. For example, Laura might receive a draft of a paper on changing weather patterns, a file named STORM.DOC from Greg (physically or over a network). After reading Greg's original text, Laura can simply change the name to STORM.TWO (or anything else) and begin to alter the original text, insert notes to Greg within the text, or write a response to Greg at the end or in another file. When Laura returns the new file (STORM.TWO) to Greg, she provides him with feedback while he maintains control of and authority over his writing, since he still has his original (STORM.DOC).

As explained earlier, most word processing programs have a feature that will divide the screen into two or three windows, each of which is able to display a separate file or a separate part of a document. Instead of using windows to revise one's own text (as suggested in Chapter 3), a reader can load another writer's text into one window and open a new file for commentary in the other window. A teacher might even provide a guidance file containing prompts for editorial comment, which can be loaded into a third window. Collaborative conferencing can also be accomplished with two or more readers sitting together sharing the same keyboard and file, one of whom may be the original author of the work.

Merging the comments from a group of readers into a single annotated text is too sophisticated for the features found in most of today's word processing programs, but this merging convenience may not be worth a separate purchase. Instead, readers can enter their comments successively, one after the other, before returning the file to the original author. To make the comments of one or more readers distinguishable from the original text, readers can write their editorial comments in a typeface that is unique, all uppercase letters for example (Rodrigues and Rodrigues 1986). Another way is to boldface the comments, causing the words to appear brighter on the screen. A third variation is to have a signature symbol precede and follow each of the reader's comments. For example, if I were reading another's text and wished to add a comment, I might chose to use the double dollar sign ($$) as my signature. (Others could choose @@;

***; &&; ++, much the way we select tokens in board games—top hats, racing cars, train engines.) Thus, my comment in another's text might look like this, with boldfacing:

> For the Massachusetts 25th that was not to be. To the common soldier, the wait between battles was tedious, but to Arrat, who before **before what? before the battle? before joining up? before in his previous daily life?** had loathed the infrequent dull moment, it was torturous. **This seems an important character trait; you might consider showing Arrat trying to deal with the torture of waiting, instead of just telling, before going on to other matters.** He got along well with the other soldiers. . . . (Original text by Ken Strickland, 1996)

With a signature symbol, it might look like this:

> For the Massachusetts 25th that was not to be. To the common soldier, the wait between battles was tedious, but to Arrat, who before $$before what? before the battle? before joining up? before in his previous daily life?$$ had loathed the infrequent dull moment, it was torturous. $$This seems an important character trait; you might consider showing Arrat trying to deal with the torture of waiting, instead of just telling, before going on to other matters.$$ He got along well with the other soldiers. . . .

Admittedly, comments designated with a signature symbol can sometimes be buried within a paragraph, but they can be found quickly by means of the search and replace function (discussed in detail in Chapter 5), a sequence that locates the next instance of a word or symbol in the text, in this case the symbol $$.

Uppercase letters, boldface highlighting, and signature symbols can also be used by the writer to draw a reader's attention to changes made in successive drafts. Similarly, a teacher could use the boldfacing feature to highlight areas to which a comment refers or areas that need elaboration. As schools acquire newer machines with more sophisticated software, teachers and students can use hypertext programs to embed messages, linking comments to the appropriate text, placing them metaphorically in stacks behind the text, like notes on index cards, messages that will appear on screen when called for with the click of a mouse.

The Next Step: Networking the Classroom

When a group of computers in a room, a building, or a school are physically linked with lengths of cable wire, similar to cable television hook-ups, they form a network and are said to be "hard wired." The limit as to how far away a computer can be and still communicate with the other computers is constrained only by the length of the cable itself. For this reason the configuration is known as a local-area network (LAN).

Michael Benedict (1995), an English teacher at Fox Chapel High School in Pennsylvania, uses a variety of local area connections to let his students conference with each other: VAX Notes, e-mail, and an integrated computer writing program. English teachers at West Morris Regional High School district have a mini-LAN configuration with peer editing circles for interaction and a software program that "allows teachers to do on-line editing and consulting, making every [computer] a potential teaching station. With one stroke on a panel, a teacher can display a student's work or model paper, and a student workstation can be used to broadcast to all the [computer] monitors in the room as well. Students can broadcast video, sound, and text through this system. They can also download data from the library without physically going there, save documents to edit in another classroom, or download work directly from home" (Kiernan 1995).

Some technical expertise is necessary to do the actual wiring and stringing of cable, but the software for a writers' network, such as those suggested in Appendix B, can be easily acquired.

The other type of network, a wide-area network, is not physically linked but makes its connections using phone lines (benefitting from fiber-optic cable) and satellite dish transmissions. This type of network has no conceivable limit. One wide-area

Chapter Four Helping Students Collaborate and Conference

network familiar to everyone is the Internet, a communications system originally created by the Department of Defense.

To take advantage of a wide-area network—to be online—a computer needs to make a connection through a modem, a piece of hardware designed to translate digital information from the computer into a signal that can be transmitted across phone lines and then translated back to digital information at the other end. When purchasing a modem, the speed of transmission is important and the general rule is faster is better. The computer itself needs a certain amount of random-access memory (RAM) and a minimum operating speed for its microprocessor, measured in megahertz, to efficiently send and receive information. A modem also allows computers to communicate with information brokers, the popular subscription services—America Online, CompuServe, Microsoft Network, and Prodigy. These services offer subscribers access to online newspapers, libraries, airline and cruise ticketing, movie reviews, and a plethora of shopping opportunities. With membership in an online information broker and a modem, my brother, Don, was able to order discounted tickets to a best-selling Broadway play before his group of teachers arrived in New York, my daughter Laura could adopt-a-whale in the name of her class while they were studying marine life, and members of a National Council of Teachers of English (NCTE) committee were able to conduct business as needed throughout the year, instead of waiting until their normal yearly meeting. The Internet and its possibilities will be discussed further in a later chapter.

The local-area network, because it is hard wired, does not require a modem, but it does need a file server, software, and interface cards. A file server is a computer that acts as the distribution headquarters, the central physical location for all the computers on the network. The software and the interface cards allow the file server to coordinate an individual's access to the network and its available software and to control the traffic flow of information and the distribution of work to printers. A LAN is attractive because it is less expensive to set up and is self-contained, but it is also limited by its wiring configuration. A wide-area net is limitless: students can write to students across the room or across the country.

Features Common to Network Software

When David Roberts (1991), of Samford University, Alabama, works with secondary English teachers as part of the National Writing Project, he shows them how to use a LAN to link up to twelve groups of writers on a network. Typically the software that creates a LAN, such as Roberts' CONFERENCE WRITER, allows groups as small as two or three students or as large as twelve to sixteen students to compose, share their writing, and read and comment on what other members of their groups have written. Software that facilitates collaborative writing also typically provides a common note pad or a shared document for students to collaboratively brainstorm, draft, edit, and share ideas. Individual writers can look at the same screen together or move independently through a document.

Some of the features that distinguish these software programs from each other are the length of the message accepted, the ability to have both private or public postings (private areas or windows for composing messages on a common topic/public windows for posting messages to all those participating in the electronic discussion), multi-task windowing to allow viewing one message while composing a reply, and the capability to do various types of searches—chronological, textual, and customized (by writer-defined links), so writers can view what a particular person has written or what has been written about a particular topic or key term. These programs also include class roster sign-ups, password protection, security traces, and activity tracking features to ensure that documents are available only to those who are authorized.

The documents themselves can be as varied as memos, proposals, progress reports and final reports, opinion papers, research papers, and letters. Some programs include online tutorials to model analysis of audience, purpose, and content.

Often the software will allow the teacher to select the protocol, or ground rules, for contributing to the document: either simultaneous, everyone "talking" at once, or more formal, turn-taking protocol. The networked screen often provides a window in which the teacher can post notices to any or all of the writers, allowing the teacher to hold an interactive editing conference while the student is engaged in composing. Terrie St. Michel (1996) found that with the computer she is literally able to talk to her students at South Mountain High School in Phoenix, Arizona. A voice-response computer program allows her to "record feedback messages to [her] students [concerning their] writings directly into the computer." She says that "being able to explain [her] editing suggestions [written on her students' papers] is a powerful instructional device." In fact, the only drawback Terrie finds is having "to spend time in the computer lab recording [her] messages" and being unable to grade "papers while waiting in the doctor's office" (4).

Posting to a Common Disk

Computers have brought with them the possibility of technological versions of the bulletin board, a common space where those with electronic access can post their commentary to a central location and view any and all notices posted by others. Helen Schwartz (1984) used this feature to great advantage with her *SEEN* program, software allowing students to share their work with classmates and to read their comments and suggestions as posted to the electronic bulletin board (see Appendix B). Teachers can replicate this sharing activity with little more than a common disk, a disk kept on reserve in the classroom or the lab (Cosgrove 1988). Students can copy files containing their latest drafts to this common disk. When students are sharing files, teachers should remind them to name their files so that they are unique and transparent (a filename using part of the student's last name, for example, would make it unique, rather than a generic name such as paper #3; a filename using three-letter extensions would make the content clear to others, PP3 for paper #3 or JR3 for journal entry #3). Students can read and reply to any and all files posted by others on the common disk.

The common disk can be used to post work in progress so that writers see, from the comments made by their peers, how others are dealing with assignments. When working with class collections, teachers must face two concerns: privacy and security. Some commercial software programs allow the teacher to eavesdrop on the writer, a practice I do not endorse, believing that any conference, whether between student and teacher or between students, should be initiated by the writer and private to the collaborating parties. Students should be free to decide when they wish to contribute to the common disk. To require that a certain amount of work or number of words be posted for all to read and respond to is a violation of the writer's privacy. Students should also be instructed in the responsibilities of writing in a community and in ways of being respectful of each other's words and feelings, so no one is hurt by thoughtless remarks (Takayoshi 1993). For this reason, I am wary of anonymous commentary. Teachers will also want to protect the disk itself from being hurt by accidental or purposeful erasure. The golden rule is Yood's "defensive computing": make back-ups (duplicate copies) of everything—files, directories, disks.

Besides collaborative contributions and replies to each other, students can write questions to the common disk about class or write comments for their teacher. While some teachers might wish to copy their responses to these questions to individual students' disks, others will want to respond on the common disk, so that any or all of the students in the class can benefit from responses to a particular student's questions.

Modeling Response

Assuming that teachers have successfully persuaded students to post their ready-for-response drafts to a bulletin board or a common disk, teachers need to spend some time modeling ways to respond to writing. Otherwise, writers receive responses such as "I liked it" or "It was good." A favorable comment is always welcome (it could have been the opposite reaction), yet students realize that "It was good" hardly says anything about the meaning that the reader constructed and is less than helpful to a writer trying to decide whether the reading was what was intended. I believe students make generic comments because they have seen little in the way of models of constructive response.

The success of any of the strategies discussed will be dependent on writers learning how to act in a community of writers. Writers need to practice strategies for how to help each other. Writers need to learn to take advice as well as give it.

There are ways teachers can support students as they learn to respond thoughtfully. Teachers and students can generate a list of questions that writers would like their readers to answer. For example, "What did you like the best (and why)?" gives a place to begin because this tells me as a writer what my reader would like to see more of. A second question could be, "How did you relate to it? Have you had similar experiences or thoughts?" because as a writer, I find it helpful to know if my reader has had experiences that correspond to what I'm writing, letting me know what I've written has significance outside my particular life. A third question might be, "Did it all make sense?" Sometimes it's helpful to know where a reader had trouble maneuvering through the text, places to which I, as a writer, can return to elaborate and clarify.

Many students are reluctant or inexperienced at suggesting what changes would make the writing better, perhaps because it seems to be playing the part of the teacher (who is perceived as always knowing what would make something better) or it means taking over the role of writer (again too presumptuous). Nevertheless, asking "What could I do to make it better?" seems to be asking the jackpot question. Basic questions such as these, or others like them, would be valuable to ask of readers, whether or not someone was using a computer. But the computer allows some variations.

The first possibility is to create a file containing a list of questions developed by the teacher and the class, similar to those above, a file named QUESTION.RSP. After reading someone else's paper, a reader could call up the file, change its name to correspond to the file that was read (e.g., a response to GATSBY.JS [a file about *The Great Gatsby* assignment by Jim S.] might be renamed GATS-JS.RSP), and answer the questions, signing the responses at the end. Readers would be free to alter the questions to suit their responses, deleting questions and adding new ones.

A variation would be to have the writer actually import the QUESTION.RSP file to the end of the written text, altering, modifying, deleting, and adding questions as the writer sees fit. A reader would then find the questions located at the end of the file. Each reader could answer the questions and save them in a renamed file, to keep the original intact, or create a collective response file by adding his or her answers to those of previous readers.

Readers could split the computer screen into two windows and load the question file in one window and the text in the other. This way, readers could use the questions as guides while making comments directly to the draft in the lower window. As long as the text file was given a different name, the original would be preserved, and the reader would be free to make comments to specific points in the text. The various software packages on the market may be more foolproof (see Appendix B), but using a word processing program to replicate the effect is less expensive and more easily customized to individual students and classes.

Reading Protocols

The Document Design Center at Carnegie Mellon University used a research technique in which they asked volunteers to read manuals and technical papers aloud and verbalize their understanding or confusion during the reading of the papers (Schriver 1984). These talk-aloud "reading protocols" would be tape-recorded and later analyzed by the writer for places in the document that would benefit from rewriting. Computers can be used to create reading protocols. Teachers can ask classmates to read one another's papers, and instead of responding to QUESTION.RSP prompts, students can be directed to boldface places where they had difficulty reading the drafts. A variation of the computer reading protocol might ask readers to summarize what the author has written by paragraph, page, or section. The writer can see where readers have difficulty and find where they may have reconstructed or misinterpreted the text. Reading protocols can be used with Peter Elbow's (1973) strategies for offering non-judgmental responses to the writing. Although Elbow and the Document Design Center have respondents talking aloud to writers, the computer offers a medium in which to record the reactions in the act of reading. This is also helpful because it gives the writer a written text, whereas in conversation, writers sometimes lose what the reader says, especially if time elapses before getting back to the writing.

Some Collaborative Assignments

Collaborative Prewriting

Stephen Marcus (1991) and Thomas Derrick (1986) suggest collaborative prewriting, where partners sit across from each other's terminal, with exchanged keyboards, acting as readers and editors for each other. For example, a student, Tom, might begin typing but his text would appear in front of his partner, Ann, on her computer screen. When Tom loses his train of thought, he has only to type, *???*, to which Ann responds with a summary of what Tom was writing about, or suggests a new angle or topic for Tom to consider.

Students can also be engaged in a directed conversation, perhaps in the form of chain paragraphs, where writers have to add or react to what was written by others and thereby discover what they think in the act of reading (or scanning). A teacher or another reader could even enter the collaborative conversation, adding a comment as simple as, "Interesting . . . I wish I knew more about how he reacted . . . ," a comment that would help a writer know what to write more about.

Group Opinion Postings

The computer can act as a place to post student opinions about matters being discussed in class. For example, Ruth Canham (1996), a secondary teacher at the Kamehameha Schools/Bishop Estate in Honolulu, has her students, during their reading of Steinbeck's *Of Mice and Men*, state their opinion about whether Candy's dog should be killed. On a related matter, Ruth also asks them to state their opinion whether Dr. Jack Kevorkian should be allowed to help people commit suicide. During free time in class, students type their opinions into the computer and are invited to read the responses posted by other students. Once everyone has had an opportunity to respond, the students read their statements and explain their relative positions. After reading what others have written and hearing the discussion, the students write a full-blown opinion paper, modifying and revising their positions according to the influence the others have had on them. The computer facilitates the social activity and the cognitive interaction.

Adolescents and young adults tend to think that everyone (except maybe their parents and teachers) thinks much the same way they do. But this exercise changes that perception. As Ruth Canham notes, "Students begin to understand how greatly opinions vary" and "see that some students justify their opinions while others state opinions with almost no support." The same strategy can be used as opinions surface in class discussion, as a way for *all* students to contribute.

The choice of Steinbeck's work isn't important; the activity can be adapted for any issue or any literary work. The opinions expressed can be collected by the computer on a class diskette, on a subdirectory on the hard drive of the lab server, on a location on a network, or through e-mail distribution. The computer acts as a way to share ideas in progress rather than fully articulated stands. The opinions can be posted by students read-

Chapter Four Helping Students Collaborate and Conference

ing the same works who may be in different classes, or have different teachers, or even be in different schools.

Collaborative Brainstorming for the Whole Class

Mary Schenkenberg (1991), of Nerinx Hall High School in St. Louis, Missouri, uses the computer for brainstorming as a whole-class activity. Schenkenberg uses a computer outfitted with a liquid crystal display (LCD) panel that sits atop a standard overhead projector. This moderately inexpensive piece of hardware creates an interactive alternative to overhead transparency technology. For example, a teacher could model a response to a work of literature, *Our Town*, for example, or by soliciting response from the class, engage the students in whole-class or group brainstorming. With a computer and the LCD panel, the responses of the students or the spontaneous drafting of thoughts by the teacher can be manipulated as a word processing file—right before the students' eyes. The computer can substitute or rearrange sentences, blocks, and paragraphs. Using a transparency or a chalkboard, one would need crossouts and arrows to show changes and connections. This strategy could be used to model any type of writing—a summary, an expository essay, a review.

Schenkenberg says, "I feel that composing together is a learning experience that is extremely valuable and difficult to achieve. For teachers and students composing together, the computer is a perfect tool" (5). Schenkenberg finds that the teacher acts as a facilitator of writing: the teacher does the typing as the responses are called out—the students do the thinking. And students learn about the process of writing: "So that's how writers think!" one of Schenkenberg's students exclaimed after a group computer session.

Collaborative Publication

Sandra Lanzoni (1996), who teaches senior English at Brockway High School in Pennsylvania, gives her students a collaborative assignment that involves the computer's desktop publishing capabilities. Following their reading of *The Crucible*, Lanzoni asks her students to form two-person teams of reporters for their own classroom-created newspaper, the *Salem Press*. The students write articles on topics of their own choosing according to Lanzoni's instructions about journalistic principles of good reporting. The computer prints rough copies to be edited by classmates.

Some students wrote stories about the "mysterious illness" that had baffled the doctors of Salem; others wrote reports about witchcraft and voodoo; still others covered the developments of the trial. The students even included obituaries and classified ads. The desktop publishing software allowed the final version of the paper to be printed right in the classroom with the appropriate newspaper format, including banners, columns, headlines, and story jumps to inside pages. Everyone in the class had a chance to participate in various roles—writers, rewrite editors, copyeditors, proofreaders, and layout designers—all aided by the computer.

Fictional Interaction Over a Keyboard or a Network

The computer can be used for a collaborative activity to teach character development in fiction, a strategy modeled on the approach used by Lee Sebastiani (1991), a teacher at the Regional Computer Resource Center, University Park, Pennsylvania.

Students create fictional characters, generating in class the elements that might help for a character sketch—age, religion, socio-ethnic background, hobbies, interests. This character sketch is stored in a separate file or given as hard copy to the teacher for safekeeping. Once the sketches are completed, students are paired at a computer and together they decide on a setting where their characters might meet, such as a school or a shopping mall. The students sharing the keyboard are asked to have their characters interact with each other according to the character traits in their sketch (neither author has previously met the other's character). For variety, or if the class has an odd number of students, the authors can have a third character join later. After the interaction, the computer prints a record of the encounter for each of the character's authors.

Students can switch partners throughout the next few weeks, meeting new characters and revisiting old ones, each time printing out a record of their meetings. As a group (the number can vary), the students construct a storyline, using the dialogue and interaction from their meetings, filling in when necessary.

The teacher and/or fellow students can use the original character sketches to decide, on the basis of the evolving storyline, how well the student stayed in character. The students should be free to revise their sketches. The variations on this interaction are endless: students can share a keyboard in the same class or be linked over a network; writers can interact with younger students or adults; the interactions can take place with characters from literature or history; the interactions can be unlikely meetings across time and space (what if Galileo met Madonna?). This fictional interaction would be especially appropriate for a creative writing class or film/theater study, but such a collaborative writing activity could enhance any class, even those in social studies or the sciences.

Computers provide technological strategies that teachers can employ to accomplish their second major task, providing response to student writings through conferencing and collaboration, while allowing writers to maintain authority of their texts. Again, computers will be valuable when used as instructional tools in the hands of teachers who understand composition theory and the writing process.

Chapter Five

Helping Students Evaluate and Edit Written Text

Editing is different from revising. If revising involves Higher-Order Concerns (HOCs), then editing involves Lower-Order Concerns (LOCs)—"concerns that deal with units of sentence length or smaller. [In editing,] the emphasis shifts from the draft as a whole to sentence structure, punctuation, usage, and spelling" (Reigstad and McAndrew 1984, 18). Editing involves getting text ready to be published. For the most part, students know how to write complete sentences and punctuate them correctly, but grammar and usage errors buried in the text on the screen escape detection. Chris Haas and John Hayes (1986) at Carnegie Mellon University found that the computer changes the process of reading onscreen; it is harder to find one's place or have a sense of where one is in a document. Yet working with typed text is also easier than working with handwritten material. Jamie Sue Crouse, a senior at Hempfield Area High School, writes that she likes "seeing my work onscreen so I can go back and read what I typed because I have the habit of skipping words when I type." Philip Andrews, also a student at Hempfield, says that he could never write as legibly as his computer types, since his handwriting deteriorates into an unintelligible hieroglyphic as his hand becomes fatigued.

Some teachers believe that their job is to teach writers to be editors; however, most of us know there is much more to the writing process. It makes more sense to support writers while they are writing, while they are making meaning, and to leave editing to be dealt with as a polishing activity that writers engage in when they are ready to display their work. If we want to help students become better and more confident writers, the time to help is during the process when writers are shaping thoughts and ideas. However, editing can and should be taught, since a correctly edited piece of writing helps a writer express thoughts clearly and in a way that is "reader friendly." So, the question is when and how to teach editing.

No matter when it is discussed, editing is more difficult than it seems. For one thing, it is hard to be one's own editor. An author is aware of the complexities and premises for a piece of writing and is not in a good position to judge where a text's mechanics might cause a reader to be confused. Students who have trouble with incomplete and run-on sentences have trouble spotting these problems when reading text for meaning. The same is true of problems with subject/verb agreement and pronoun/antecedent agreement. Instead of using workbook exercises, writers need strategies to help them look at their own sentences the way an editor does. To edit, one needs to step back from the writing and read with a fresh eye. Someone else, a peer, a teacher, can help give advice for editing. Writers can work in pairs with teachers, tutors, or other students, checking each other's work for run-on sentences, incomplete sentences, agreement errors, and sentence variety.

However, asking someone else to read our writing can cause another problem of editing. Unless we are clearly asking someone else to read for "correctness," response to grammatical concerns or mechanics can feel like criticism to the writer or even dismissal of what the writer was trying to express. In any case, if someone has to criticize their work, most students would prefer to have their teacher do it rather than their fellow classmates. The students feel that the teacher will know what each writer should do to correct the piece (to get a good grade), while the other students will be equally confused about what to do and give advice of dubious worth (in terms of bettering a grade). Perhaps the students are right; they have had little training as editors, other than reading something and saying, "That's nice."

The students in each writing group need to be shown editing and evaluating strategies so they can offer each other valuable advice. We need strategies for acting in a community of writers—suggesting ways to help each other edit—and the computer can help by providing assistance at the "correctness" level. When using the computer to copy edit, there are several functions employed by most word processing programs that make editing easier.

Using Spell Checkers

When students speak of their writing, they are often most anxious about the correctness of their spelling. Katie Stewart, a junior at Hempfield Area High School, tells me, "Instead of using a dictionary, I just use the spell check command and my computer highlights all the misspelled words and offers alternatives." Classmate Kelly Dzendzel concurs, "For proofreading, I have found something that I cannot imagine living without—spell check. I find it amazing that incorrectly spelled words appear immediately and the computer suggests choices as to the correct spelling." Several years ago, a professor at another university asked my opinion of spell checkers. In reply to my comment that I thought they were helpful, she countered, "I never let my students use them; I make them use a dictionary." Perhaps she misunderstood the dictionary's purpose. Dictionaries are useful for explanations of a word's meaning, pronunciation, and linguistic history. Dictionaries are less than helpful for spelling, unless you already know how to spell a word.

Justin Marinos, a senior at Hempfield, writes, "I can clean up almost any of my papers by deleting errors, making grammar and spelling corrections, and changing my diction—all with the use of a computer. . . . If a word is misspelled by only a few letters or even if the word [only] remotely looks like the desired words, the computer will pick up on it, asking whether or not the word needs [to be] changed and, if so, gives suggestions to change it." A spell checker on a computer employs a master list of words taken from a dictionary, using a matching protocol to see if a given string of letters constitutes a pattern-match with any of the words on its list. Spell checker inquiries do not bother with meaning, pronunciation, or linguistic history.

Another student at Hempfield, Amber Stuver, makes the point humorously by lauding the spell checker's ability to let her concentrate on composing instead of spelling. "To illustrae [sic] my point I have left my paper unchecked to this point (yes, I did see those mistakes)." Because of the spell checker on her computer, Amber has the luxury of ignoring LOCs in favor of concentrating on HOCs, knowing she can attend to spelling concerns when the time is right.

Spell checkers usually include a thesaurus feature that allows writers to check for suggestions of alternate words, synonyms, or antonyms for the word highlighted by the cursor. Diane Persin, a junior at Hempfield, believes the thesaurus feature of her word processing program makes her compositions "more entertaining" and "expands my vocabulary while I write." She adds, "While skimming through some old rough drafts from the past few months, I discovered that I have learned over two dozen new words."

Teachers should caution students against wholesale replacement of words for variety's sake. Not all word processing programs include a definition with the words suggested by the thesaurus. My word processing program gives lists of comparable words. For example, for *experienced*, it offers *accomplished* as one of its substitutes, and for *accomplished*, it offers *brilliant*. An *experienced* writer may or may not be *brilliant*. The word processing program I used two years ago provided a definition for each word its thesaurus suggested, along with its part of speech. More experienced writers know that each word has its own nuance; less experienced writers must learn this by broadening their reading, not by computer lists.

A spell checker is not infallible and teachers need to make students aware of the feature's limitations. Spell checkers are like seat belts: they have to be used to be useful. I have seen many student writings extolling the wonders of spell checkers containing words that are obviously misspelled (perhaps the student used the spell checker on an earlier draft instead of the last one). Hempfield senior Kristi Romas notes, "If you use the wrong form of a word, but spell it correctly, [the spell checker] does not tell you of your error." Similarly, spell checkers are not case sensitive; they won't catch uncapitalized initial words in a sentence, provided they are spelled correctly. Justin Marinos warns, "Sometimes the [spell checker] picks up on a word that is not in its dictionary, so the computer automatically assumes the word is misspelled." He adds that proper nouns are particularly troublesome. Spell checkers will also pass over words that are correctly spelled but not actually the word intended. If Amber Stuver had typed ". . . unchecked to this pint," the spell checker would respond, "remaining words okay." Homonyms are also worrisome: *weather* for *whether*, for example. A student would be better off typing *wether* because the spell checker would suggest both alternate spellings, *weather* and *whether* (and four others), asking the student to make the choice. Spell checkers make the writer responsible for the replacements of flagged words, and isn't that what we want our writers to be, responsible for their text?

Using Style Checkers

A variety of commercial software packages will give students additional information about their writing style. Style checkers, as they are known, will process text and analyze it for certain features. Frequently, popular word processing programs include a style checker feature, eliminating the need to purchase separate software.

Some packages will figure the average sentence, word, and paragraph length. Hempfield junior Katie Stewart says that "the grammar check on my computer . . . highlights all sentences that may not enhance my paper and suggests different ways to write them. For instance, any sentence written in the passive voice would be brought to my attention as would any with a redundant phrase. Run-on sentences and fragments are also identified." Some will give a graphic representation of sentence length, sentence by sentence. The tacit message is to use a variety of sentence lengths. Style checkers will identify the number of *to be* verbs, the instances of passive voice, and the use of vague terms. Most style checkers give the reading level of the text based on standard indexes such as the Gunning Fog index, suggesting that writers not exceed the reading level of their target audience. To arrive at their readability count, most style checkers are sensitive to the number of polysyllabic words and the length of the sentences. A text with a reading level of 12.5 has a significant number of "big words" and longer sentences than one with a reading level of 7.6. A style checker would predict that the 12.5 text is harder to comprehend and therefore requires a higher level of education. Critics of style checkers delight in running a selection from a famous writer such as Plato, and point to the readability level, something between a 4.0 and a 6.0 perhaps, knowing that the text would be incomprehensible to a sixth grader. The opposite results could be achieved with an elementary school text that used long sentences and funny polysyllabic words. Imagine a third grader being given a book with a twelfth grade readability level. Yet, if students are aware of what style checkers are sensitive to, then the readability numbers will not be so confusing and can be used to suggest examining word choice and sentence length.

Teaching students to edit using a spell checker and a thesaurus is mainly a matter of teaching them to be careful in adopting the computer's suggestions. Teaching students to edit using style checkers is more tricky. The wealth of information offered by these packages compounds the assortment of advice that students have to attend to. Teachers need to give students strategies for responding to advice concerning average sentence, word, and paragraph length, *to be* verbs, instances of passive voice, and the use of vague terms, while still making sure that student writers retain control over their text and its meaning.

What to Do with Statistics

I asked the style checker packaged with the word processing program I am using to examine my draft of this chapter thus far.

It told me that the average sentence length of my ninety-one sentences was 19.9 words, a length it found most readers could easily understand. It told me that the average word length of my 1,837 words was 4.92 letters and 1.58 syllables, a length most readers would be comfortable with, based on syllables per word. The style checker told me that the average paragraph length of my fifteen paragraphs was six sentences, a length most readers could easily follow. The Gunning Fog index was 14 and the Flesch-Kincaid grade level was 11, a score that represented six to ten years of schooling, a level it felt would make my text difficult for most readers.

At this point in the analysis, I was confused. The style checker seemed to say that statistically my levels were good but my text was difficult to read. I had a similar experience going to the doctor and finding out the tests performed showed that my levels were all within normal range, while I was still sick. Neither the doctor nor I had a clue what to do next. Students will undoubtedly have similar experiences.

I pressed on with the style analysis, asking for specific advice. The message I received was "scanning for first error," a remark that I took as discourteous but not offensive. Nevertheless, my first error was identified as a run-on sentence because I had used too many conjunctions in one sentence. Technically, the sentence wasn't a run-on; it lacked gracefulness. Would students know the difference? The style checker suggested dividing the sentence into two or more sentences, but it didn't suggest where to make the cut.

The next error flagged was one of many instances of passive voice. My style checker directed me to a handbook explanation of passive voice—"The ball was thrown by Joe"—but left me on my own as far as restructuring my sentence. I decided that I didn't want to make the "actor of the action" apparent because that would alter what I was trying to express. Would students know the difference?

The next error wasn't actually an error. In the appositive used to identify Jamie Sue Crouse, the style checker told me the singular subject, *senior*, takes a singular verb, not the plural verb, *school*. The style checker considered *school* to be a verb, and it recommended making *senior* plural. Would students know enough not to act on the suggestion?

The next case in point involved the style checker's belief that, despite the lack of a period, an "end of a sentence" was constituted by my mistaken use of the enter key to move to the next line of text, instead of allowing word wrap to fill the lines to the margin. The hard return was misinterpreted by the style checker, and its advice was to use a capital letter for the first word of a sentence, although the "first word" was actually in the middle of a sentence, one already capitalized and punctuated with a period. Would students understand what caused the confusing advice?

The phrase *less experienced writers* was marked to be replaced by the phrase *fewer experienced writers*. Would students know which was correct? Several more instances occurred where the style checker incorrectly identified errors in subject-verb agreement and homonym confusion.

Every one of my seventeen long sentences, ones containing over thirty words, was considered to be in need of trimming. Earlier I had been told my average sentence length was fine, but seventeen times I was told contrary information. The style checker hadn't told me that my thirty-one short sentences, ones containing fewer than twelve words, were too short. I chose to ignore the warning. Would students begin to lose patience?

There seems to be no way to predict what information will be given by the style checkers and what percentage of the information will be accurate and valuable. I would suggest that students use the style checkers in groups of two or more, so they have someone to discuss the advice with. I would also suggest teachers submit a piece of their own writing to be analyzed before the class to demonstrate how the statistical information and advice given by style checkers must be filtered through the writer and the writer's intentions. (Later in the chapter, specific collaborative editing strategies will be discussed, which might be of help as students learn to support each other as peer editors.)

A Minilesson on To Be *Verbs*

Many style checkers will count the number of *to be* verbs used in a writer's text—*is, was, were, will be, are*, etc. (the one I'm using does not). Students might wonder why style checkers would care how many *to be* verbs appear in their writing. What could be wrong with *to be* verbs? These verbs hide the action in nouns and are little more than statements of existence, verbal equivalents of mathematical equations: X is Y; Y is Z; thus, X is Z. "The cost of most cars today is over $20,000; I think cars that cost over $20,000 are too expensive. As you can see, cars are too expensive." One or two statements of fact are acceptable, but teachers can use the highlighting ability of the style checker to suggest that students change some of their writing by discovering where the *to be* verbs are. "The cost of most cars today is over $20,000" can be rewritten as "Most cars today cost over $20,000." The commercial software will locate the instances of *to be* verbs, but will not offer a strategy for the more difficult editing task of rewriting the sentences.

Teachers may approach this task of dealing with *to be* verbs in a minilesson similar to the demonstration of responses to the style checker's statistics. Using a volunteer's paper, the teacher could demonstrate how the computer identifies the *to be* verbs and, with the class, consider ways to rewrite the sentences, debating the relative benefits of competing versions.

I encourage students who have an abundance of these verbs to look at the words that follow the verb to find a word that might make a better verb. For example, "Spending federal money on nuclear power plants is a waste of our limited tax dollars" can be improved by looking at the words after *is*. The term *a waste* can be used as the verb *wastes* to transform the sentence into, "Spending federal money on nuclear power plants wastes our limited tax dollars." Students might object that this change is nothing major; the two sentences mean the same thing. Yet, the computer may be enough of an authority to convince students of what professional writers and writing teachers have been saying for years: nothing puts life into writing more than action verbs.

Conversely, nothing robs life from writing more than *is* verbs, turning writing into formulas: "everything is everything, and something is something else."

The computer may be enough of an authority to help writers identify possibilities, but editing decisions remain the province of the writers themselves. Computers will not teach editing, but students can learn about editing with computers. Teachers may find some of the following strategies helpful to students who are in the process of becoming better writers.

Sentence Separation as Editing Strategy

The sentence separation strategy, discussed as a revising strategy in Chapter 3, allows writers to notice a host of things when concentrating on Lower-Order Concerns, and may be helpful as an editing strategy. For example, I have been guilty of writing some awful sentences; I excuse myself by saying that I simply didn't notice the nominalizations, the split infinitives, the unclear referents, the passive voice, and the obtuse constructions. I was so concerned with generating material and constructing my argument that these faults escaped detection, buried as they were in the text on the screen. Fortunately, using the sentence separation strategy, the computer enables writers to evaluate each sentence in isolation from what precedes it and what follows to get a sense of how well each sentence is functioning on its own. Take, for example, sentence variety. Are all sentences approximately the same length? (under ten words? over twenty words?) Do they all begin the same way? Do they all have an introductory phrase before getting to the subject and predicate? Do they begin with words like "and," "but," "so"? I have students who like to begin sentences with "Well, . . ." in the mistaken belief that it lends a conversational tone to their writing. Unfortunately, obviously conversational writing sounds odd to the reader, unless it's dialogue between characters.

The sentence separation strategy allows writers to notice how well the sentences move forward from old to new information, according to the functional sentence perspective of Gregory Colomb and Joseph Williams (1985). Colomb and Williams believe that the early part of a sentence should refer to information already given in a text; the known information then leads to the new information given in the sentence. For example, the last sentence in the preceding paragraph was originally written as, "Unfortunately, writing sounds odd to the reader when it tries to be obviously conversational." The "conversational tone" was the known information (from the preceding sentence), but I had placed it last in the sentence. I rewrote the sentence to move from known to new: "Unfortunately, obviously conversational writing sounds odd to the reader, unless it's dialogue between characters."

After examining the sentences in isolation, writers have the choice of putting the sentences back in place or returning to their original untouched file, as they did when using sentence separation as a revision strategy.

Using Search-and-Replace

Most word processing programs have a function known as search-and-replace, a function that directs the computer to look through a text and pick out any sequence of letters that a writer has requested. The sequence doesn't even have to be a word, although it often is. For example, a student writing a paper on *ethnology* might misspell it as *ethology* all the way through the paper (which the spell checker wouldn't catch, since *ethology* is a word) or occasionally mistype it as *ethology*. The writer could call up the search function (using a function key) and type *ethology*. Then the writer could call up the replace function (another function key) and type *ethnology*. The third step would be to direct the computer to do the search, based on the option chosen—replacing words throughout the text automatically or replacing one word at a time at the writer's confirmation. The writer could also request a part of the word in the search sequence. For example, the writer might have asked the computer to replace *ology* with *nology* or *eth* with *ethn*. Of course, taking shortcuts such as this could have amusing results. The first search could replace *biology* with *binology*, and the second search could replace *method* with *methnod*.

Extensive typo replacement is the most common use for the search-and-replace function, but this function can be used to teach an editing strategy. Search-and-replace can be used to scan text for problematic words. I have trouble with overuse of meaningless words in my drafts such as *very* and *really*. Before I consider my text as finished, I use search-and-replace to check for the use of *very*, one instance at a time. If I find it in a sentence, I try to rewrite the sentence, communicating the intensiveness of *very* but eliminating the word itself. For example, if I were writing directions for changing a lighting fixture in the house, I might warn, "Removing the old fixture may be very dangerous if you neglect to turn off the power at the fusebox." The word *very* adds little to the information. Using the search-and-replace function, the computer would highlight the sought-after word and offer me the option of deleting the word (my suggestion), replacing it with another word (I might be tempted to write "*really* dangerous"), or rewriting the sentence.

Search-and-replace can be used to scan for words the teacher or the writer considers problematic. I suggest that students search for what I call "fuzzy" words: *very*, *really*, *quite*, and *rather*. I ask them to search for excessive *which* phrases and suggest they replace them with free modifiers, as discussed in Chapter 3. I have students look for words that begin with *th-* such as *this*, *these*, and *there*, and I suggest that they consider replacing these words, which are frequently little more than placeholders or dummy subjects of sentences. For example, in an earlier draft I wrote, "There is often a window provided on the networked screen where the teacher can post notices to any or all of the writers . . ." If I searched for instances of *there*, I could show students how *there* is a placeholder for *window* and rewrite the sentence as, "A window is often provided . . ." The style checker would notice that the sentence is in the passive voice and I could rework the sentence further, "The networked screen often provides a window . . ."

I also ask students to look for nominalizations by looking for words that end in *-ion*, and I suggest turning the nominalizations back into active verbs. For example, "The confusion is the result of different computer platforms . . ." can be rewritten as "Different computer platforms confuse . . ."

As with many of the LOC strategies, students may object that they do not perceive any difference in the reconstructed sentences, regarding the changes as further instances of the arbitrary nature of English. Teachers should spend time finding a way to frame the difference. For example, many people enjoy watching the diving competitions during the summer Olympics, and other than applauding when the television commentator prompts them, few understand what distinguishes one dive from another. Many attribute the points awarded to the arbitrary nature of judging. However, the dives differ in terms of style, grace, economy of movement, preciseness of movement, and control, much the way alternative versions of sentences differ from one another. Judgment has to do with experience and therefore expertise. More experienced writers are able to see stylistic differences in execution.

Each of these editing strategies can and should be taught within the context of the students' own writing, using the search-and-replace abilities of the word processing program. The decision for actually editing the piece of writing always remains the students' responsibility and choice.

Printing and Desktop Publishing

One of my students once told me that she liked writing with computers because "even if I don't like what I wrote, I know it looks good at least." Controlling the printing of a document, producing what is now known as hard copy, and considering layout options give students a reason for paying attention to editing. Using desktop publishing to publish class collections, literary yearbooks, programs, and entries for authors' awards banquets exert a powerful pressure to make sure a piece of writing "looks good." Most word processing programs have layout, font, and appearance menus, allowing students to control details that used to be the domain of printers and artists. Today students' papers can look more like pages from a book or a journal instead of dot matrix printouts or purple ditto copies.

Collaborative Editing

One way to encourage students to pay attention to editing and to build confidence in their editing skills is to have them work in non-threatening collaboration activities. Several of the following activities involve groups editing with the computer, engaged in game-like competitions, which may have points or prizes awarded as teachers see fit.

The Great Punctuation Game

The first editing game is the Great Punctuation Game, adapted from Pat Hartwell (1978) and Elray Pedersen (1991). Students use the search-and-replace function to remove periods, extra spaces between sentences, commas, and semicolons from their writing (using a duplicate file so the original is preserved). Next, students mark their text and ask the computer to convert case so all the words are in lowercase letters.

At this point, the game begins as students trade their text with partner. Students attempt to restore punctuation to the texts that they receive in the trade. When finished, they compare their punctuated version with the original. Each correct mark of punctuation in the new version receives a point; punctuation not in the original, which the author agrees to use, receives double points. Who scores more points becomes a forgotten issue as students begin interesting conversations about punctuation.

Hartwell's version of the game strips punctuation from professional pieces of writing taken from a variety of news and entertainment magazines. Teachers might enter these types of articles into text files and use them for an interesting variation on the computer punctuation game.

Replace-the-Verb Game

The Replace-the-Verb Game requires that pairs of students once again trade copies of their writings. Working with their partner's file, students use the computer's cursor to move through the text one word at a time. At each verb, students try to replace the verb with a more sensory appealing word (some say substituting strong verbs for weak verbs). Students score a point for each verb replaced. Students are given double points for replacing *to be* verbs: *am, are, is, were, was, will be*.

Extra Sentence Game

The Extra Sentence Game, adapted from an interactive activity designed by Jeff Golub (1994) requires a triad of writers.

In the original activity, Jeff gives his students a passage from *Animal Farm*, telling them that he has added a sentence that wasn't in the original. Their task is to decide which is the extra sentence. Students playing the Extra Sentence Game (which could be done individually or in groups) take a piece of writing done by the first member of the triad, and the second member of the triad adds one extra sentence per paragraph (or page). When finished, the second member passes the new version to the third member of the group. The task of the third member is to identify the sentence and mark it for deletion. If the third member spots the correct sentence that was added, a point is awarded. If an original sentence is deleted, the second member gets the point and the writer of the original text gets to keep the new sentence, if so desired. After struggling to read and detect the extra sentences, the class can discuss what they have discovered about text coherence and redundancy.

As a variation of the same activity, students are given a sample piece from an earlier class so each student is working with the same material. Every writer has sentences that basically repeat what has already been said, without adding anything new. A variety of extra sentences will be detected, and a discussion will follow. Following this activity, I tell my students about editors, people whose profession it is to spot and delete these sentences; editing is an honorable profession.

Replace-a-Pronoun Game

The Replace-a-Pronoun Game is much like the other collaborative games. The task involves trading papers as before, but this time asking each partner to replace ten personal and relative pronouns in a draft. Points are awarded for each instance where the original author agrees the specific noun is clearer than the pronoun in the draft.

A variation could be offered as a class enterprise, based on a creative fiction lesson of John Heyn (1991). Heyn gives his students the following scenario: "He left. She laughed. Their loft. That's life." Heyn asks his students to replace the pronouns and write the story that goes with it. Teachers can use Heyn's script or construct their own, such as: "This job. My mother. I wept." or "Her smile. His look. She cried. He closed his eyes."

The variations on these editing games are endless. Students can be directed to add verb phrases to their papers or their partner's papers. They could be challenged to make the independent clauses into dependent clauses, while maintaining complete sentences. They can be asked to search for passive voice constructions and rewrite sentences. By changing the target of the activity, greater fluency with editing can be taught. Teachers can use any or all of these editing activities as deemed needed by the writers, not as meaningless activities to kill class time or as a series of "mastery exercises" to be completed. By making editing a game, a spirit of collaborative fun rather than hierarchical criticism can be cultivated. The computer makes the searching and the substituting relatively easy to accomplish. The writers remain the decision makers.

Chapter Six

The Final Frontier: Cyberspace on the Internet

Inevitably, writing teachers who use computer technology must turn to the Internet. Though its technicalities and jargon are daunting to many, the change from a linear chronological orientation to a multi-directional spatial orientation causes the greatest adjustment. Though one *reads* the screens on the Internet, it has less in common with a book than it does a telephone or television. With a book, a reader moves sequentially from first to last page, moving through an implied chronological narrative. With a phone or a television, one simply dials the correct number (often on a touch-tone keypad) to ring a phone in a location that conceivably could be anywhere or enters the channel number on a "clicker," the television's wireless remote. The Internet, like these other technologies, is organized according to space—one disconnects and dials another number anywhere in the world or jumps to another channel. The difference is that phone numbers and television's cable channels have no relationship with other numbers and channels. Imagine if the MTV channel had a link to another channel, VH-1, to which one could jump with a click of a button on the remote. Locations on the Internet have relationships to other locations, links by which a user can jump from one location to the other merely by pointing the remote (in this case, a mouse) to the link on the screen and clicking one of the buttons on the mouse. So computer users, like telephone users who care little about the switching mechanisms and the fiber optics that make phoning possible, can use their knowledge of these other twentieth-century communication devices to understand the Internet's point-and-click operation.

Those who use the Internet mix their metaphors with abandon, though most of them have to do with exploring space: crawling along the Web, traveling the information highway, surfing cyberspace, and navigating hyperspace. Cybernauts on the Internet, who sometimes feel as though they are "lost at sea," have programs called network browsers or navigators (Netscape, Microsoft Explorer, Mosaic) that act as a metaphorical Traveler's Aid Station or Auto Club, offering maps, roadside assistance, and ticketing services to get explorers where they want to go.

Net Addresses

In a landmark ruling concerning freedom of speech on the Internet, the Federal courts called the Internet "a never-ending worldwide conversation." Like all conversations, Internet talk is prone to jargon, metaphors, and acronyms. Continuing the space exploration metaphor, places to visit on the Internet—locations variously known as sites, home pages, chat rooms, and multi-user dimensions (MUDs)—have addresses called URL addresses (Universal Resource Listings). Internet addresses use slashes and dots (what used to be called periods) to separate elements in addresses, just as phone numbers are written with parentheses and dashes: (412) 555-1212. The addresses are written to refer to the computer that sponsors, hosts, or holds the information stored on its directories, supplying other details for pathways to the specific information sought. My university's previous URL was sruvm.sru.edu (the first block of information is the name of our computer in Maltby Hall; the second block is the abbreviation for our university; the third block identifies us as an educational location). The address has been shortened to sru.edu. Some other location types are commercial (com), non-profit organization (org), government (gov), and military (mil). URL addresses are confusing at first but no more than if I were to write my postal address as an Internet address. It might look like this: *slippery_rock.pa/126.applewood.lane/jstrickl.*

If my URL is listed on the World Wide Web (a mega-directory of who's where on the Internet), then the address would begin with *www.* and users would signal that they'd like to go to a URL location by beginning the address with the special code *http://* (standing for hypertext transfer protocol). Thus, my university can be visited on the World Wide Web by giving this address to the browser: http://www.sru.edu. My publisher can be visited at this address: http://www.heinemann.com (Heinemann, a commercial publishing enterprise).

If the Web traveler doesn't know an address, the Internet has search engines, the equivalent of directory assistance. With the click of a button on the browser screen, one can engage a search engine, such as Lycos, Yahoo, or WebCrawler, to look up addresses that match a given descriptor. The process resembles doing a search of the Education Resources Information Clearinghouse (ERIC) database or using the subject-heading cards in the Library of Congress card catalogue.

Presently, visiting Internet sites resembles looking at pictures at a museum exhibition. Most are text-based with graphics of less-than-photographic quality. Net surfers read a large quantity of text, though more often they scroll through the text, checking for pertinent information, catching the crest of the wave rather than submersing themselves in it. A new languaging program, Java, will soon make the Internet interactive. Sites will no longer be static pictures and text; they will contain animation, sound, video images, and dialogue capabilities.

Until then, users communicate by writing letters to persons at the various Internet sites, letters known as e-mail (electronic mail). When I was in college, I wrote letters to my parents and my girlfriend; our daughter never wrote when she was in college, she phoned. Today kids are writing again, this time on the Internet.

The addresses for e-mail are similar to the Web addresses, except senders need to answer the question, "With whom do you wish to speak?" The answer is expressed as so-and-so at (@

symbol) such-and-such address (written in lowercase letters). The industry standard is becoming an eight-letter name made up of a first initial and the first seven letters of the person's last name. Sometimes companies reverse the order and use seven letters of the first name and a last initial. One might predict that my e-mail address would be jstrickl@sru.edu or perhaps jamess@sru.edu. However, my university has decided to use an address system spelling out full first and last names. Thus, my e-mail address is james.strickland@sru.edu. The Internet encourages creativity and individuality. It won't be long before we see vanity tags on the information highway.

Inappropriate Material

Once on a wide-area network, some teachers and undoubtedly their students will want to venture into cyberspace to make new friends, have new adventures, learn, and explore. Teachers will experience the sensation parents have when their children leave for college, worrying about their welfare, their choices, their wisdom. But as everyone knows, if you raise them right . . .

Teachers need to be honest in offering advice about making wise choices involving the available services and the people they will meet on the Internet. Unfortunately, the advice is usually that since transactions on the Internet are not secure, students should not reveal anything personal on the Net (not even their name) while engaged in online conversations, should not give out credit card information over the Net, should not attempt to enter sites marked "18 or older," and should not attempt to download copyrighted files or information (security code hackers may look glamorous in movies, but in real life the penalties are severe).

Home Pages

The joke behind the popular *Wayne's World* comedy was that two teenage "head-bangers" would somehow be allowed to host their own public-access cable program broadcast from their basement. Students today can have Wayne's virtual world by creating their own home pages on the Internet. A home page, or a Web page, is a site with its own unique address on a host computer, a place to visit. The home page has information to offer (reports, reviews, opinion papers, FAQs—answers to frequently-asked-questions) and graphics to show (photos, artwork, drawings, designs).

Faculty members in my department have been creating their own home pages, where they offer listings of their educational degrees, their complete course syllabi, course assignments, and bibliographies of their publications (sometimes with complete text). I have seen some who include personal histories and photographs.

Our mother used to advise us never to write anything we'd be embarrassed to see printed on the front page of the Buffalo Evening News. The same advice holds true here; I would hesitate to publish anything on a home page that I might not want everyone in the entire world to know—personal information about my children, for example, and what "frequently censored books" might appear on my reading lists. When students are required to create home pages, I would be even more careful about the privacy issue. Students and their parents may not be aware that everyone in the world—from convicted felons to prizewinning authors—is able to look at what is posted.

Home pages also offer the possibility to make links to other locations on the Internet. For example, I could include connections to other sites of interest to me professionally—sites connected to courses (Aristotle's rhetoric home page or the Whole Language home page), my publisher's home page, professional organizations such as NCTE—and sites of interest to me personally—The Cousteau Society home page or the Bob Dylan home page. One member of our faculty has a link on her home page to her brother's home page, encouraging others to visit him at college, on the Internet.

The Credibility Issue

Some Internet users feel the home-grown personal home pages "make the Internet democratic because anyone with a computer can share what's important to her with the world" (James-Catalano 1996, 36). "Some people share their political views, others their favorite hobby, but most importantly," James-Catalano continues, "people have an outlet that really hasn't existed before. (How many people can afford to publish their own newspaper or produce their own TV show?)" (36). This sharing of information is one of the key benefits afforded by the Internet. Some find personal home pages invaluable because their creators write about subjects that are personally important to them: "these pages tend to be comprehensive and often contain more information than 'official' sites" (James-Catalano 1996, 36). A recent article in *Newsweek* described the proliferation of home pages offering advice from and for people suffering from any one of a multitude of debilitating and sometimes life-threatening diseases (Hafner 1996). Anyone who has had a loved one suffering in a hospital, and has had experience trying to catch doctors on rounds to ask them questions, will appreciate the answers to FAQs found on Internet home pages (from advice offered by those participating in interest groups). The *Newsweek* article even revealed that sometimes the person at the other end of the computer is a medical doctor, surfing the Net during down times at home or at the hospital. Sometimes the person isn't a doctor; however, and the advice offered might be potentially harmful.

The problem I have been worried about for years, one the *Newsweek* article acknowledges in its concluding paragraph, is that there's no way to tell who is or is not an authority on the Net. To author tends to give one authority, a point we concede in the expression, "so-and-so wrote the book on that!" In cyberspace, anyone can claim authority, posing as one who knows things, presenting information in a format identical to those whom others would consider experts. Stories on the Associated

Press news wire or printed in the *New York Times* can be taken as credible; stories in the *National Enquirer* are generally considered entertainment rather than news. On the Internet, fringe groups and academic scholars have the same standing; everyone looks the same. No imprimatur validates published information with a seal of approval.

Research Helpers

When I was in college, I was aware that term papers could be purchased on a variety of topics. I assumed that my teachers could tell a professionally produced term paper from one written by an earnest student such as me. Today, teachers need to be aware that there are "homework" services available on the Internet. Commercial Web sites offer to provide reference materials for high school students who need citations from reputable information sources, notably articles from major encyclopedias and full text articles from hundreds of magazines. I can only assume that the term paper–helpers are also online.

Last year, my brother, Don, had two students in his class at Penfield High School, New York, who chose to create a web page on the Internet to fulfill part of their project requirements for the final assignment in eleventh grade English. My brother had no way of knowing how reliable the students' facts and sources were, although the students gave references for their work, according to the MLA-style form of citation now being standardized for electronic sources (Walker 1996: http://www.cas.usf.edu/english/walker/mla.html). He had his suspicions when the students wrote about President Kennedy's Cuban missile crisis at the Bay of Pigs. Did the students simply download information that was bad? Did they misinterpret what they had read? And once written, would anyone visit their site and begin to rely on their information as correct?

My brother was also bothered by the fact that the students seemed to spend more of their energy creating the Web page than synthesizing the research they downloaded and writing the

Chapter Six The Final Frontier: Cyberspace on the Internet

text. He didn't know if the students actually submitted their home page address to various search engine companies, which they would need to do to have anyone who didn't already know their address locate them on the Web. If they did submit the paperwork, choosing descriptors that would classify their creation, other students could conceivably reproduce their information, mistaking the student authors for historians, unless they had clearly identified themselves as students. And since anonymity is part of the fun of the Internet, who wouldn't be amused if the students indulged their imaginations and created personas for themselves?

When Don's students characterized President Kennedy as one of America's most moral presidents, their citations pointed to Internet documents. Admittedly, an equally over-enthusiastic opinion of our president could be gotten from a book in the library, but books in libraries are published for the most part by companies with reputations to protect. A fringe group, a white supremacist group, for example, could publish a home page, hypothetically calling it something like True American Information Resource Server, that would, to the novice Web user, appear to have the same rank and status as the legitimate educational Native American Information Resource Server (http://www.afn.org/~nativ/) created by Carolyn J. Edds (cited in James-Catalano 1996, 36).

If material is published by Heinemann-Boynton/Cook, teachers have some assurance that the information is sound—editors have checked the lines of argument and the references cited and endorse the editorial stance; copyeditors have verified facts and references; and legal advisors have verified that there is nothing libelous in the text and permissions for quotations have been granted. Information published by lesser known houses, vanity presses, and independent publishers should be considered as speculative. Personal home pages should be viewed in the same light.

One well-intentioned teacher, Carolyn Cole, created a home page she calls the *Busy Teachers' Web Site* to offer teachers links of helpful sources on a variety of subjects (http://www.gatech. edu/lcc/idt/students/cole/proj/k-12/toc.html) (cited in James-Catalano 1996, 37). The only problem with this helpful site is Cole's disclaimer: she is not responsible for information found at any of the sites that she provides a link to, and she does not certify that the information is accurate. Hypothetically, right-wing extremist groups could set up Web sites to promote any of their educational beliefs in the guise of a "teacher's helper" home page like Cole's and provide links to other Web sites that they find sympathetic. Their underlying agenda need not be identified. Even worse, Cole could make a link from her *Busy Teachers' Web Site* to any of these without being aware of the potential harm.

Cyberwriting

With all those cautions in place, the Internet offers some liberating possibilities to teachers. One teacher who has gotten her students excited about reading and writing is Robin Bucaria, the chair of the English department at Monument Valley High School in Utah. Robin's seventh through twelfth grade students are students on a Navajo reservation in San Juan County, a part of the United States so remote Robin needed a guide to find her way there from Alaska after she had taken the job four years ago. The Internet, to Robin's students, is the gateway to the world. So anxious are her students to enter this world that Robin says she has seventh graders begging to stay after school to work on their Web pages. By visiting Monument Valley High School's home page (http://www.mvhs.sanjuan.k12.ut.us), Internet surfers can learn about Navajo culture and write to ask questions; Robin's students answer the inquiries as the experts.

Robin Bucaria (1995) saw an opportunity to use the Internet "to build the ultimate reading and writing workshop," allowing her students to share their work and receive "feedback from students from across the United States and the world" (1). Robin taught her students simple hypertext markup language (HTML) so that they could create their own home pages featuring visual,

Chapter Six The Final Frontier: Cyberspace on the Internet

aural, graphic, and written material about themselves, their hobbies, tastes, and favorites. Robin believed this project would develop "reading, writing, thinking, and computer technology skills . . . [because it] requires that students find, generate, represent, and organize information while considering their audience and finding ways to engage their audience" (1).

As part of her Cyberwriting project, all seventh graders who have parental permission will link four to six pieces of writing to their Web page. Robin is sensitive to the privacy issue of posting work on the Internet. She has found that the parents of some of her best writers have decided not to grant permission to put their children's work on the Internet. Robin noticed that these students come from the more traditional Navajo families, but she has been unable to detect any violation on her part of cultural traditions or teachings. She respects the parents' wishes and has taught the students how to write HTML code and how to design a Web page but has not required the students to post their writings.

Robin's students welcome communication from any Internet users, but in particular, they are posting their work to students from an exchange school located within the United States, exchanging information about their school, community, customs, and lives. Last year, Robin piloted the project with a high school in Columbus, Georgia, using the U.S. Postal Service.

Robin's students have been busy producing travel writing, essays, and narratives, and their writing (and any accompanying videos and photographs) is sent to the students from the exchange school via the Internet. When the exchange school sends similar items from their schools, the students at both schools receive a practical geography lesson with unique insights from teenagers who live in each area.

One of Robin's assignments that benefits from being online is her version of the I-search Paper, a research paper based on student interest, interviews, observations, real-life experiences, as well as traditional research techniques (Macrorie 1988). A critical component of the I-search paper is the personal interview, and Robin suggests that her students conduct the interview over the Internet by using e-mail or by joining appropriate news groups. Students can send a message stating their topic and specifying what kind of help they want. Internet information resources (libraries, topics, etc.) can also be investigated using a variety of search engines. Robin suggests exchanging completed I-search papers with students from other schools through an electronic bulletin board. Other students could respond through e-mail correspondence over the Internet.

Students also have a wealth of new information sources not available to them in their local library or school library. That can be a boon and a curse. Robin believes that students who engage in their own research on the Internet develop critical thinking skills because they are confronted with the question of how one finds truth, especially on the Internet. Carol Jago (1996), an English teacher at Santa Monica High School, found herself overwhelmed by the information offered to her by the Department of Defense's home page, BosniaLINK, the Web site that handles information about the NATO peacekeeping mission to Bosnia (http://www.dtic.dla.mil/bosnia/). BosniaLINK contains statistics, fact sheets, troop deployment information, maps and charts, news releases, photos, biographies, transcripts of meetings, speeches, and testimony—data upon data. Carol warns her students that they will encounter "all the facts a laptop strategist could desire," but they should be prepared to be "overwhelmed by drivel." Carol tells her students that authors, journalists, reporters, and historians need to weave facts into a coherent story. She decries "information masquerading as insight" and argues that information must be "framed by narrative" (B5).

Students can engage in a variety of activities besides research over the Net. With Internet conference groups, Robin says "students could create short stories, poetry, or essays and send their writing to a bulletin board and get comments" (2). Teachers would need to monitor "to make certain that constructive criticism is happening—that students praise, question, and help produce a final copy of each piece of writing. Final copies could be published through an electronic literary magazine (Gala-Global Author's Literary Anthology)" (2). Students could correspond with published authors and prepare their own book talks, "hypermedia presentations on books they read, sharing them over the Internet" (2). Students can become linguistic investigators, studying language as it is used on the Internet. Cordelia Kohrman (1995), an English teacher at Shepherd High School in Michigan, adds another Internet activity—using cyberspace to investigate and apply to colleges. Her students find home pages for colleges and follow the links to learn about course offerings, admission requirements, financial aid, and any unique features of a particular campus. Kohrman's students are often able to correspond with current students and graduates to learn insider information about a campus.

Professional Activity

Many professional organizations are making member services available on the Internet. NCTE has made progress toward offering Net services to its members, through the efforts of Cindy Selfe, Gail Hawisher, and Tharon Howard and the Instructional Technology committee. One of the problems the organization and its committees have encountered has been finding a campus or organization to host and maintain the home page on its computer. The Instructional Technology committee has been conducting its year-long business through a listserv, an electronic memo distribution list, sponsored by Clemson University, Tharon Howard's university. Years earlier, Helen Schwartz was able to create a bulletin board where members of the executive committee of NCTE's Conference on College Composition and Communication (CCCC) did business between semi-annual meetings. As these electronic committee meetings become more commonplace, teachers online will feel more and more connected to others in the profession.

Those unable to attend a professional conference meeting may be able to attend an online version of the conference. As an online complement to the 1995 CCCC meeting held in Washington, D. C., CCCC Online "made available online convention information, including the texts of the convention preview and the convention program; abstracts of presentations; electronic mailing lists; and real-time online meetings, including a number of MOOs [real-time discussions online]" (Hawisher et al. 1996, 251). One of the hopes of holding virtual conferences in conjunction with the physical meeting is that the technology will serve "as a means of bringing marginalized groups into more central positions, permitting those without status, salary, and travel funds to participate [more fully] in the profession" (251).

Brian Monahan (1995) adds three other professional activities teachers can engage in: chatting with other English teachers, conducting research at libraries online, and searching for a job (5). Any number of forums can be subscribed to, a phrase that means joining a discussion group rather than paying a membership fee. Monahan gives the example of a forum on language arts operated by the Carey School of Education at the University of Virginia (state.virgina.edu). He suggests visiting the Library of Congress for the research (locis.loc.gov) and searching the *Chronicle of Higher Education* for a new job (chronicle.merit.edu).

Professional publications are another possibility on the Internet. Presently, a number of electronic journals are being planned for English teachers; however, funding remains a problem. Since most of the cost of publishing a professional journal is accounted for by the printing and the mailing costs, an electronic journal could be more cost-effective—if one could entice enough people to pay a subscription fee. Offering an electronic version of a print journal at no charge on the Internet could mean the end of the print version. If some professional research publications were to be offered over the Internet in online formats, for example the annual *CCCC Bibliography of Composition and Rhetoric*, the resources would be more widely available to English teachers. At the same time, those who have been purchasing the paper editions from publishing houses, for example the CCCC annual from the Southern Illinois University Press, would be faced with increasingly higher costs as the subscription base shrinks. The utopian dream will be freedom of information and information for free, but the reality will be that someone has to pay for the salaries of those who enable publishing to occur.

Distance Learning

Some advocates of technology speak of the virtual classroom, a classroom without physical location, one created by virtue of teachers and students being linked on a network. Many people are offering courses online through the Internet. These courses present text-based lectures (soon they will be videotaped lectures or even live-action lectures), which students will dial up and read or watch. The instructor will post assignments and examinations. Writing teachers will probably make sure that students interact with each other through various real-time communications such as MUDs and MOOs, computer equivalents of getting together after school in the cafeteria or at the student union ("Please pass the virtual doughnuts"), or through listservs, the computer equivalent of putting everyone in class on a memo distribution list. Students in computer-enhanced writing classes will still interact in ways described in Chapter 4, regardless of the distance involved in the computer collaboration. I'm not so optimistic that other academic disciplines will resist the pull back to the traditional transmission delivery mode of education. The Internet could radically change our notion of education as a place, a physical location—Bishop Neumann High School or the University of California at Berkeley—where people go to meet other like-minded people to participate in courses of study. There have already been advertisements placed in computer magazines for distance learning. Distance Instruction for Adult Learning (DIAL) is now being offered by an organization calling itself the New School in New York City, whose home page can be visited at http://dialnsa.edu/home.html. Conceivably, home schooling could become the norm, and every student could connect to the National High School site, downloading a national curriculum. O brave new world . . .

Conclusion

Technology is changing so rapidly that any conclusions about the use of computers in the English classroom are necessarily tentative. Nevertheless, it is fairly certain that school boards and taxpayers will continue to approve funding for the purchase of computers. It is also certain that those groups will be clueless as to how computers should be used in the classroom. It will be the teacher's job to make informed decisions about the role technology plays.

The introduction of technology enhances some aspects of its context, while repressing other aspects. "Technology, then, brings inherent values, amplified values that users of technology accept knowingly or less so" (4), claims Don McAndrew (1995), a former high school English teacher and professor of English Education at Indiana University of Pennsylvania. Some object that the curriculum is being usurped by software developers, despite advertising claims that their software has been developed with the *help* of *active* teachers. Frank Smith (1988) asks, "Who will make the decisions that determine how children learn, teachers working directly and collaboratively with children, or 'programmers' pulling the strings from the outside?" (91). McAndrew worries that the computer views learning as the acquisition of objective data bits while it discounts the understanding of language as "a social and cultural reality constantly reconstructed by the community of . . . individuals-in-society" (8). McAndrew hopes we will accept technology, but "accept it on our terms," reiterating the "importance of student-centered classrooms," the artistic and intuitive nature of reality, and the proactive responsibility of teachers in the classroom (9).

The question will not be whether to use computers but how to use them. Their use will determine their value. If English teachers keep their eyes on learning rather than on information

Chapter Six The Final Frontier: Cyberspace on the Internet

acquisition, we will have a better sense of what to do with computers. Teachers will be able to use computers to support writers, offering strategies that would be impossible or unlikely without the technology. My hope is that we, as teachers and researchers who understand composition theory, will apply our best practice to the use of computers in the writing classroom.

Appendix A

Glossary of Computer Terms

Block. A means of highlighting text in order to modify it in some way, such as changing its type style (causing it to appear boldfaced or in italics), changing its font, copying, moving, or deleting it from the document.

Boldface. An attribute enhancing the appearance of text, causing the marked text to appear brighter on the screen and darker in print.

Browser. A program that allows users to navigate or move through the Internet using hypertext links. Most browsers, such as Netscape and Microsoft Explorer, are graphics based, which means that they will display artwork and sound as well as text.

Chat rooms. A virtual space located in a computer's memory where various groups of people can meet and interact in real time.

Copy/move. One of the most important features of word processing, the copy/move sequence allows writers to cut and paste their words. It involves marking a block of text and, depending on which keystroke sequence is chosen at the end of the marking, duplicating the text elsewhere or physically moving the text to another location in the document.

Appendix A Glossary of Computer Terms

E-mail (electronic mail). Messages sent from one computer on a network to another computer on the same network or on a linked network, such as the Internet. E-mail requires communications software, so that computers can speak to each other, and computer addresses, which include the party to be reached and the computer at which the party may be reached.

FAQ. A hypertext document linked to a home page used by the owner of the home page (or the "Webmaster," as these people responsible for maintaining web sites refer to themselves) to post answers to frequently-asked-questions about the topic of the home page.

File extension. In DOS-based systems, the three-letter part of a filename following the dot, usually designating the type of file, for example, .SYS for a system file, .DOC for a document, and .EXE for a file that can be run as an application.

File server. A central computer on a hard-wired network that stores files so that computer users can share the same software programs and communicate with each other.

Hard copy. A printout. Hard copy refers to the physical existence of the document as opposed to a virtual on screen/on disk existence.

Home page. A site, or a Web page, with its own unique address on a host computer, a place to visit. The home page has information to offer (reports, reviews, opinion papers, FAQs—answers to frequently-asked-questions), and graphics to show (photos, artwork, drawings, designs).

HTML. A computer acronym for hypertext markup language, the computer code that allows documents and home pages to exist on the Internet. HTML tells the computer how to display the text and graphics on the screen in terms of size, location, font, color, and intensity.

HTTP. A computer acronym for hypertext transfer protocol, or the directions for how to search the hypertext links in order to find the document requested in the address following the *http://* command.

Hypertext. The non-sequential arrangement of small units of text-based information linked in collected groupings (or webs). In hypertext, some words are "hot"; that is, users can jump from that word to a linked unit located elsewhere on the web.

Import a file. To retrieve a file from stored computer memory and introduce it into active computer memory; for example, into a document currently being written.

Java. A computer language that allows Internet sites to be interactive. Documents and home pages can be more than static pictures and text; they can contain animation, sound, video images, and dialogue capabilities.

Local-area network. A physically linked grouping of computers in a room, a building, or a school—hard wired—to share software, information, and printers. A LAN (its acronym) uses a file server for distribution of software programs and print jobs and interface cards to coordinate access and distribution of work. Less expensive than a wide-area network, a LAN is limited by its wiring configuration.

Links. Buttons, colored words or images, that are hot, signaling a place to go in a hypertext document. Users can choose to follow the hypertext link by pointing to the button and clicking their mouse.

Log on. A computer expression that means to start an application software program (boot up) and identify the user by some sort of password.

Appendix A Glossary of Computer Terms

Modem. A hardware device that allows a stand-alone computer to connect to other computers on a network, sending (uploading) and receiving (downloading) information.

MOO. A computer acronym for MUD, Object-Oriented (see MUD entry). A more sophisticated form of a Multiple-User Dimension that, in addition to real-time discussions online, allows the creation of virtual objects, including virtual versions of the players. The objects are created in text by the individual users, and others at the MOO can request a description of and interact with any object in the room. For example, when I log on at a MOO location, I can give myself a name (a real name or a *nom de plume*), and create a description of myself and any other objects that I wish to take with me. I could take my dog with me, creating a virtual (text-based) description of Patty the dog. Others at the MOO could "look" at Patty (get a description of her), and perform an action, such as waving to her or giving her a virtual biscuit.

Mouse. A peripheral device that complements the computer keyboard as an input device and connects to the computer by a thin cable that metaphorically resembles the tail of a small animal. Rather than entering information with keys, computer users can roll the mouse across a pad, thereby moving the pointer on the computer screen, and click one or more of its buttons to select menu items and enter commands.

Move. See Copy/move.

MUD. A computer acronym for Multiple-User Dimension. A MUD is a virtual room or location where computer users (or "players," as the people online sometimes refer to themselves) can meet to have a real-time discussion with others who are present (as opposed to communicating via e-mail).

Navigators. A family of browsers (Netscape, Microsoft Explorer, Mosaic) or navigation programs that allow users to move in hyperspace. Each navigator has a series of features that users can click to carry out an operation. For example, clicking on the search button will engage various search engines and clicking on the bookmark button will record the address of the site currently being visited, providing a shortcut similar to memory speed-dialing on a telephone.

Network. A collection of computers, linked either by cable wire as a local-area network or by modems and phone lines such as the Internet, that shares information and peripheral devices, such as printers.

Renaming the file. To change the name of a file in active memory and thereby create a duplicate file, since the original file is still saved in the computer storage memory.

Saving the file. To write the contents of a file in active memory to a storage device, such as a hard drive or a disk.

Scrolling. To move up or down through pages in a document with the help of arrow keys or a mouse.

Search-and-replace. To move quickly to a word, phrase, or symbol in a document and to replace it with another word, phrase, or symbol, if so desired.

Search engines. Devices used to retrieve information about sites on the Internet (URL addresses with brief annotation). Search engines, such as Lycos, Yahoo, Magellan, Excite, or WebCrawler, generally catalog specific information within a narrow range of topics. Users can repeat searches for different engines, or they may use meta-search engines that combine the resources of the individual search engines or may use a Wide Area Information Search (WAIS) for more complete coverage.

Sound card. A hardware device plugged into the computer's main circuits (motherboard) that allows the computer to repro-

Appendix A Glossary of Computer Terms

duce vocal or musical sounds. With a sound card, a user might be able to hear the sound of a hummingbird's wings while viewing a graphic image of the bird or hear John F. Kennedy delivering his inaugural address while viewing the text of the speech.

URL. An Internet address, sometimes decoded as "Universal Resource Listing" or "Uniform Resource Locator."

Virtual. To be without physical existence, created by virtue of being simulated in computer memory or over a network.

Wide-area network. A limitless number of computers linked by phone line connections (using twisted pair cable and fiber-optic cable) and satellite dish transmissions. To connect to a wide-area network—to be online—a computer engages a modem, hardware designed to translate the computer's digital information to an analog signal transmittable across phone lines, which is then translated back to digital information at the other end. A modem allows computers to communicate with information brokers, the popular subscription services—America Online, CompuServe, Microsoft Network, and Prodigy—and to employ network browsers to locate sites on the Internet, such as Netscape Navigator and Microsoft Explorer.

Window. To split a computer screen into separate areas, each of which is a window, to be able to view separate parts of a document or multiple documents on the same screen.

World Wide Web. Sometimes referred to as "the Web," the organization of URL locations on the Internet whose addresses begin with "www." Metaphorically analogous to a spider's web, the World Wide Web permits browsers to locate sites on its directory in a non-linear search mode (rather than a linear, hierarchical search).

Appendix B

Examples of Representative Software

A. *Software to Help Writers Generate Ideas*

Daedalus Invent

Daedalus Invent evolved from the original computer invention programs written by Hugh Burns (1980) at the University of Texas. *Invent* offers prompts—based on Aristotle's topoi, Burke's pentad, and Young, Becker, and Pike's tagmemics—designed to help writers systematically explore their topic. Writers can print, save, and export their responses to a word processing file. Teachers can create additional questions and customize the prompts to suit specific classes/assignments. (Available separately or as part of the *Daedalus Integrated Writing Environment* software package.)

Daedalus Group, 1106 Clayton Lane, Suite #250-W, Austin, TX 78723. (800) 879-2144. http://www.daedalus.com/

Fine Lines (IBM/MS-DOS only)

Fine Lines is subtitled *Planning, Drafting, and Revising on the Computer*. Its seven modules reflect a recursive model of writing, allowing users to move from invention strategies (freewriting, focusing, and listing) to outlining, drafting, and revising strategies. *Fine Lines* includes a journal module, using single- or double-column format.

Houghton Mifflin/McDougal-Littell/D. C. Heath, One Beacon St., Boston, MA 02108. (800) 733-2828. http://www.hmco.com/trade/

Inspiration

Inspiration is a planning program that includes three functions: brainstorming (to graphically map free-associated ideas), diagraming (to create visuals, flow charts, technical diagrams and tree charts), and writing (to turn the brainstorm sessions into written outlines). Brainstorm and diagram sessions can be imported and exported; outlines can be imported and exported to popular word processing software programs.

Inspiration Software Inc. (formerly Ceres Software), P.O. Box 1629, Portland, OR 97207. (503) 245-9011. http://www.inspiration.com

Learning Tool (Macintosh only)

Learning Tool is a hypertext program developed by Robert Kozma and John Van Roekel of Arborworks. *Learning Tool*, described as an electronic notebook, allows writers to make note cards and build relationships between concepts at various levels of abstraction. The screen actually looks as though it has note cards spread out on it, and the writer has the option of searching and organizing the notes, picking one up to read, and/or continuing to write.

Distributed by Intellimation, P.O. Box 1922, Santa Barbara, CA 93116-1922. (800) 346-8355. e-mail: intelllfm@aol.com

Paradigm® Online Writing Assistant©
(Web site)

Paradigm® Online Writing Assistant© is an interactive, menu-driven, online writer's guide and handbook written in HTML and distributed freely over the World Wide Web. The program's advice, accessible through hypertext links, is drawn from current composition and rhetoric theorists such as Maxine Hairston, Peter Elbow, Edward Corbett, Kenneth Burke, James Britton, and Stephen Toulmin. Paradigm's main menu offers advice organized according to type of essay: informal, thesis/support, exploratory, and argumentative, and stage of writing: discovering ideas, organizing, revising, editing, and documenting sources. Paradigm was developed by Chuck Guilford of Boise State University with the help of his late brother Tom Guilford.

Paradigm Web site address, http://www.idbsu.edu/english/cguilfor/paradigm/

Storyspace

Storyspace is a hypertext program for writing that facilitates invention, drafting, arrangement, presentation, outlining, mapping, and linking of text. STORYSPACE was developed by Jay David Bolter, Michael Joyce, and John B. Smith.

Eastgate Systems, 134 Main Street, Watertown, MA 02172. (800) 562-1638. http://www.eastgate.com

Success with Writing

Success with Writing is a comprehensive writing process package, using the PACE system: Prewrite, Arrange, Compose, and Evaluate. Its Prewriting module, in addition to freewriting and brainstorming, contains an invisible writing module that blanks the screen. The Compose module lets users draft either with or without the notes and outlines from the first two modules.

Scholastic, P.O. Box 7502, 2931 East McCarty Street, Jefferson City, MO 65102. (800) 541-5513. http://www.scholastic.com

Writer's Helper: Prewriting and Revising
(Software)

Writer's Helper is an integrated software package for writers developed by William Wresch, offering prewriting activities (finding a topic, examining the topic from different perspectives, and organizing the ideas generated) and revising activities (examining the structure of a document, looking at audience considerations, and checking for problem words). *Writer's Helper* includes an export link to popular word processing software programs.

Appendix B Examples of Representative Software

New Horizons, 1912 F Street, Iowa City, IA 52240. (800) 365-9774. e-mail: kcdaiker@aol.com

B. Software to Help Collaborative Revision

Common Space

Common Space offers writers the opportunity to coauthor, comment, and collaborate on a shared text by generating an expandable series of individual columns as annotation workspaces referenced to an original column of writing. Collaborators can edit duplicate copies of text and view the changes made in context, can hide or collapse text and columns, and can even record voice annotations, conferencing in real time over local-area networks or the Internet. *Common Space* includes question sets to guide collaborative response and a library of frequently used comments to facilitate response.

Sixth Floor Media, 222 Berkeley Street, Boston, MA 02116. (800) 565-6247. http://www.sixthfloor.com/

Daedalus Respond

Daedalus Respond is an evaluation program that prompts users to read and respond to online peer drafts by dividing the screen into three windows, one displaying the text, another asking a guiding prompt, and the third providing a note pad for critical response. Teachers can create additional questions and customize the prompts to suit specific classes/assignments. (Available separately or as part of the *Daedalus Integrated Writing Environment* software package.)

Daedalus Group, 1106 Clayton Lane, Suite #250-W, Austin, TX 78723. (800) 879-2144. http://www.daedalus.com/

SEEN: Tutorials for Critical Reading

SEEN features six authorable tutorials for examining a particular subject—character analysis, plotting in literature, essay analysis, exploratory essays, art exploration, and historical conflicts—in order to develop and support a thesis. Developed by Helen

Schwartz, *SEEN* includes bulletin boards that accompany the tutorials. Through the bulletin boards, students can read and comment on the work of their peers and receive reactions to their own work, comments necessary to revise for a real audience.

New Horizons, 1912 F Street, Iowa City, IA 52240. (800) 365-9774. e-mail: kcdaiker@aol.com

C. Software to Help Writers Collaborate over a Network

Aspects (Macintosh only)

Aspects provides a shared workspace for collaborative groups of two to sixteen students to brainstorm, record, and edit ideas into a common document. *Aspects* allows students to look at the same screen together or scroll independently through the document. It also allows the instructor to set the protocol for contributing ideas—simultaneous contribution or a more formal turn-taking protocol.

Group Logic, 1408 North Fillmore Street, Suite 10, Arlington, VA 22201. (800) 476-8781. http://www.grouplogic.com

Collaborative Writer (Macintosh only)

Collaborative Writer teaches writers how to approach projects and work with other writers on workplace tasks such as memos, progress reports, final reports, feasibility studies, and proposals. Developed by Ann Hill Duin of University of Minnesota, *Collaborative Writer* provides online tutorials to model analysis of audience, purpose, and content.

Research Design Associates, 35 Crooked Hill Road, Suite 200, Commack, NY 11725. (800) 654-8715. http://www.rda.com

Daedalus Classmanager

Daedalus Classmanager controls the entry of users onto a network system, provides password protection and security traces, man-

Appendix B Examples of Representative Software

ages network writing documents, and handles many routine DOS functions. (Available separately or as part of the *Daedalus Integrated Writing Environment* software package.)

Daedalus Group, 1106 Clayton Lane, Suite #250-W, Austin, TX 78723. (800) 879-2144. http://www.daedalus.com/

Daedalus Interchange®

Daedalus Interchange® offers real-time (synchronous) text-based discussion to facilitate whole-class or small-group conferencing. Students compose messages on private windows and send those messages to classmates for immediate response by posting them to public windows. The discussion can be searched chronologically, textually, and by writer-defined links. (Available separately or as part of the *Daedalus Integrated Writing Environment* software package.)

Daedalus Group, 1106 Clayton Lane, Suite #250-W, Austin, TX 78723. (800) 879-2144. http://www.daedalus.com/

Daedalus Mail

Daedalus Mail is an electronic mail (e-mail) program designed for local-area network classrooms, offering features such as sending messages drafts or responses to individuals (classmates or teacher) or members of a collaborative group. Offers private and public postings and windows to allow viewing one message while composing a reply. (Available separately or as part of the *Daedalus Integrated Writing Environment* software package.)

Daedalus Group, 1106 Clayton Lane, Suite #250-W, Austin, TX 78723. (800) 879-2144. http://www.daedalus.com/

Realtime Writer 2.0

Realtime Writer provides up to forty separate discussion channels for interactive discussion. *Realtime Writer* includes a window for composition and a window for users on an individual channel to read all the comments that have been sent as part of the ongoing dialogue. A third window is provided for the teacher to post notices to any or all of the channels. The software behind the ENFI Project (Electronic Networks For Interaction), *Realtime*

Writer includes password security, class roster, and activity tracking features.

Realtime Learning Systems, 2700 Connecticut Ave., N.W., Washington, DC 20008-5330. (800) 832-2472. (No Internet address available.)

D. Software to Help Writers Document Research

Daedalus Bibliocite®

Daedalus Bibliocite® collects bibliographic information, compiling it into both a database of sources and a list of references for a research paper in either the APA or MLA bibliographic styles. (Available separately or as part of the *Daedalus Integrated Writing Environment* software package.)

Daedalus Group, 1106 Clayton Lane, Suite #250-W, Austin, TX 78723. (800) 879-2144. http://www.daedalus.com/

Documentation Hotline

Documentation Hotline is an online pop-up guide to styles of referencing. For each of the four major styles of documentation, including MLA and APA, the *Hotline* explains listings of works cited, parenthetical and endnote in-text documentation, and appropriate page layouts. Available only as an ancillary to St. Martin's Press and Bedford Books handbooks.

St. Martin's Press, 175 Fifth Avenue, New York, NY 10010 (800) 446-8923. http://www.sfo.com/%7esisson

Nota Bene (IBM/MS-DOS and Windows only)

Note Bene is a word processing program designed for scholarly writing, including automatic footnoting, page numbering, generation of tables of contents, lists of illustrations, bibliographies, and indexes. *Note Bene* features keyboard adaptions for all major Western European languages and special supplements for non-Western European languages.

Appendix B Examples of Representative Software

Nota Bene, 285 West Broadway, Suite 460, New York, NY 10013. (212) 334-0445. http://soho.ios.com/~notabene

Pro-Cite

Pro-Cite is a utility program for creating bibliographies, offering a wide variety of formats for record types and style sheets, and providing sorting, searching, and indexing capabilities.

Research Information Systems, 2355 Camino Vida Roble, Carlsbad, CA 92009-1572. (619) 438-5526. http://www.pbsinc.com

The Research Helper (Macintosh only)

The Research Helper contains two programs: *Notefiler*, designed to store and sort information collected and compiled for a research paper; and *Documenter*, a guide for writing bibliographic entries, in MLA or APA format.

Harcourt Brace, 301 Commerce Street, Suite 3700, Fort Worth, TX 76102. (800)-237-2665. http://www.harcourtbrace.com

E. Software to Help Writers Analyze Style

Edit! (IBM/MS-DOS only)

Edit! checks documents written with its own internal word processing program and documents generated by other programs. *Edit!* has four levels: word, sentence, and paragraph levels and an overall level for checking topic and concluding statements for sentence length, variety, and idea development, asking "post-write" questions and displaying statistics.

McGraw-Hill, 11 West 19th Street, New York, NY 10011. (800) 262-4729. http://www.mcgraw-hill.com

Editor (IBM/MS-DOS only)

Editor is the Modern Language Association's stand-alone, menu-driven style and usage checker. Developed by Elaine and John Thiesmeyer, *Editor* reads and analyzes errors in punctua-

Appendix B Examples of Representative Software

tion, mechanics, and spelling (non-standard spellings and colloquialisms not caught by most spell checkers) using four separate usage dictionaries—*Fix, Tighten, Polish*, and *Consider*.

Distributed by TASL, Box 8202, North Carolina State University, Raleigh, NC 27695-8202. (800) 955-8275. e-mail: pas@aip.org

Grammatik 5

Grammatik 5, available separately in earlier versions, is now bundled with WordPerfect® word processing software. *Grammatik 5* reads text, comparing each word against its collection of rules for grammar, style, punctuation, and spelling, offering interactive advice and suggestions for revision. *Grammatik 5* provides statistical information about the readability levels of the text as well as about the paragraph, sentence, and word counts. Judgments can be adjusted according to business or technical and general or informal writing styles.

Corel, 1600 Carlington Avenue, Ottawa, Ontario, Canada K1Z 8R7. (800) 772-6735. http://www.corel.com

Grampop (IBM/MS-DOS only)

Grampop is a memory resident program designed to provide answers to questions about grammar and usage. The program is modeled on and contains specific references to the *Harbrace College Handbook*.

Harcourt Brace, 301 Commerce Street, Suite 3700, Fort Worth, TX 76102. (800) 237-2665. http://www.harcourtbrace.com

Writer's Workbench® 5.0 (Unix only)

Novell's *Writer's Workbench®* is an educational version of the style checking program developed by AT&T Bell Laboratories and tested at Colorado State University. *Writer's Workbench®* includes programs whose names indicate their focus—Organization, Development, Findbe (locates forms of "to be" verbs), Diction & Suggest, Vagueness, Spell, Check (for troublesome pairs such as *affect/effect*), Punctuation, Grammar, Prose (comparisons), Style (analysis), and Abstract (words or phrases). *Writer's Workbench®* provides statistical information about a student's writing but leaves the decisions about changes to the writer.

EMO Educational Software, Inc., 1250 Shore Road, Naperville, IL 60563. (708) 369-1350. http://www.emo.com

References

Benedict, M. 1995. E-mail correspondence, December 15.

Blau, S. 1983. "Invisible Writing: Investigating Cognitive Processes in Composition." *College Composition and Communication*, 34: 297–312.

Bucaria, R. 1995. "Cyberwriting: A Star Schools Curriculum Proposal." Unpublished grant proposal.

———. 1996. E-mail correspondence, April 1.

Burns, H. L. 1980. *A Writer's Tool: Computing as a Mode of Invention*. ERIC: ED 193 693.

———. 1984. "The Challenge for Computer-Assisted Rhetoric." *Computers and the Humanities*, 18 (3/4): 173–181.

Canham, R. 1996. Personal correspondence, January 16.

Christensen, F. 1978. *Notes Toward a New Rhetoric: Nine Essays for Teachers*. Rev. ed., ed. B. Christensen. New York: Harper & Row.

Colomb, G. and J. Williams. 1985. "Perceiving Structure in Professional Prose." In *Writing in Nonacademic Settings*, ed. L. Odell and D. Goswami, 87–128. New York: Guilford.

Cosgrove, N. 1988. "Conferencing with Computers." *CSSEDC Quarterly*, 10 (3): 5–6.

Cowden, J. 1996. Personal correspondence, February 14.

Dauite, C. 1986. "Physical and Cognitive Factors in Revising: Insights from Studies with Computers." *Research in the Teaching of English*, 20 (2): 141–159.

Derrick, T. J. 1986. "DOSEQUIS: An Interactive Game for Composition Students." *Computers and Composition*, 3 (2): 40–52.

References

Elbow, P. 1973. *Writing Without Teachers*. New York: Oxford.

Flower, L. 1979. "Writer-Based Prose: A Cognitive Basis for Problems in Writing." *College English*, 41: 19–37.

———. 1985. *Problem Solving Strategies for Writing*. New York: Harcourt Brace Jovanovich.

Golub, J. N. 1994. *Activities for an Interactive Classroom*. Urbana, IL: NCTE.

———. 1996. Telephone conversation, July 18.

Guth, H. 1988. "Revitalizing Composition: The Unfinished Agenda." Promotional literature for *The Writer's Agenda*. Belmont, CA: Wadsworth.

Haas, C. and J. R. Hayes. 1986. "What Did I Just Say? Reading Problems in Writing with the Machine." *Research in the Teaching of English*, 20: 22–35.

Hackett, J. 1991. "Poetry with Graphic Highlights." In *The English Classroom in the Computer Age: Thirty Lesson Plans*, ed. W. Wresch, 49–53. Urbana, IL: NCTE.

Hafner, K. 1996, May 27. "The Doctor Is On." *Newsweek*, pp. 77–78.

Hartwell, P. 1978. "The Great Punctuation Game." *Freshman English News*, 7 (1): 16–17.

Hawisher, G. E., P. LeBlanc, C. Moran, and C. L. Selfe. 1996. *Computers and the Teaching of Writing in American Higher Education, 1979–1994: A History*. Norwood, NJ: Ablex.

Heide, A. and D. Henderson. 1994. *The Technological Classroom: A Blueprint for Success*. Toronto, Ontario: Irwin.

Heyn, J. 1991. "Using Computers to Write Fiction." In *The English Classroom in the Computer Age: Thirty Lesson Plans*, ed. W. Wresch, 32–34. Urbana, IL: NCTE.

Jago, C. 1995. "Using the Shift Key for a Power Shift." Unpublished manuscript.

———. 1996, January 31. "War on the World Wide Web." *Los Angeles Times*, p. B5.

James-Catalano, C. N. 1996. "Creation and Order." *Internet World*, 7 (1): 36–38.

Kiernan, H. 1995. E-mail correspondence, December 13.

King-Shaver, B. 1996. E-mail correspondence, January 29.

Kohrman, C. 1995, Winter/Spring. "Let's Go Gophering, or Computers, Telecommunications and the World." *ACE Newsletter*, p. 4.

Lanzoni, S. 1996. Personal correspondence, March 19.

LeBlanc. P. 1993. *Writing Teachers Writing Software: Creating Our Place in the Electronic Age*. Urbana, IL: NCTE.

Macrorie, K. 1988. *The I-Search Paper: Revised Edition of Searching Writing*. Portsmouth, NH: Boynton/Cook.

Marcus, S. 1984. "Realtime Gadgets with Feedback: Special Effects in Computer-Assisted Writing." In *The Computer in Composition Instruction: A Writer's Tool*, ed. W. Wresch, 120–130. Urbana, IL: NCTE.

———. 1991. "Invisible Writing with a Computer: New Sources and Resources." In *The English Classroom in the Computer Age: Thirty Lesson Plans*, ed. W. Wresch, 9–13. Urbana, IL: NCTE.

McAndrew, D. 1995. "Computers, Values and Teaching English: A Mismatch of Theory and Politics." Unpublished manuscript.

Monahan, B. 1995. Winter/Spring. "Internet Activities for English Teachers." *ACE Newsletter*, 5.

Murray, D. M. 1984. "Writing and Teaching for Surprise." *College English*, 46 (1): 1–7.

Paterson, W. 1988. "Sentence Examination Using the Word Processor." *CSSEDC Quarterly*, 10 (3): 4–5.

References

Pedersen, E. L. 1991. "Computer Writing Warm-Ups." In *The English Classroom in the Computer Age: Thirty Lesson Plans*, ed. W. Wresch, 17–26. Urbana, IL: NCTE.

Porter, W. 1996. Personal correspondence, January 17.

Reigstad, T. J. and D. A. McAndrew. 1984. *Training Tutors for Writing Conferences*. Urbana, IL: NCTE/ERIC.

Roberts, D. H. 1991. *Conference Writer* [computer program]. Birmingham, AL: Samford University.

Rodrigues, D. and R. Rodrigues. 1983. *Creative Problem Solving* [computer program]. Fort Collins, CO: Colorado State University.

———. 1986. *Teaching Writing with a Word Processor, Grades 7–13*. Urbana, IL: NCTE/ERIC.

Rose, M. 1980. "Rigid Rules, Inflexible Plans, and the Stifling of Language: A Cognitivist Analysis of Writer's Block." *College Composition and Communication*, 31: 389–401.

St. Michel, T. 1996. "Using Computers to Enhance Student Writing." Unpublished manuscript.

Schenkenberg, M. 1991. "Modeling the Literary Paper." In *The English Classroom in the Computer Age: Thirty Lesson Plans*, ed. W. Wresch, 3–5. Urbana, IL: NCTE.

Schriver, K. A. 1984. *Revising Computer Documentation for Comprehension: Ten Exercises in Protocol-Aided Revision*. CDC Technical Report No. 14. ERIC: ED 278 943.

Schwartz, H. 1984. *SEEN* [computer program]. Iowa City, IA: Conduit.

———. 1986. *The Student as Producer and Consumer of Text: Computer Uses in English Studies*. ERIC: ED 283 211.

Schwartz, M. 1982. *Prewrite* [computer program]. Roslyn Heights, NY: Learning Well.

Sebastiani, L. 1991. "Imaginary Worlds." In *The English Classroom in the Computer Age: Thirty Lesson Plans*, ed. W. Wresch, 59–61. Urbana, IL: NCTE.

Selfe, C. and B. Wahlstrom. 1983. *Wordsworth II* [computer program]. Houghton, MI: Michigan Technological University.

Shaver, J. P. 1990. "Reliability and Validity of Measures of Attitudes Toward Writing and Toward Writing with the Computer." *Written Communication*, 7 (3): 375–391.

Simmons, K. 1996. Personal correspondence, March 1.

Smith, F. 1988. *Joining the Literacy Club: Further Essays into Literacy*. Portsmouth, NH: Heinemann.

Spitzer, M. 1984. *Brainstorm* [computer program]. Old Westbury, NY: New York Institute of Technology.

Strickland, J. 1984a. *Free* [computer program]. Slippery Rock, PA: Slippery Rock University.

———. 1984b. *Quest* [computer program]. Slippery Rock, PA: Slippery Rock University.

———. 1987. "Computers, Invention, and the Power to Improve Student Writing." *Computers and Composition*, 4 (2): 7–26.

———. 1989. "How the Student Writer Adapts to Computers: A Protocol Study," *Computers and Composition*, 6 (2): 7–22.

Strickland, K. 1996. "The Story of Arrat Mont." Unpublished essay, Penfield High School, NY.

Takayoshi, P. 1993. "Women and E-mail: Issues of Gender and Technology." *English Leadership Quarterly*, 15 (2): 7–10.

Von Blum, R. and M. Cohen 1984. *WANDAH (Writing-Aid and Author's Helper)* [computer program]. Los Angeles, CA: UCLA.

Walker, J. 1996. "MLA-Style Citations of Electronic Sources." http://www.cas.usf.edu/english/walker/mla.html. March 24.

References

Winterowd, W. R. 1975. *Contemporary Rhetoric: A Conceptual Background with Readings*. New York: Harcourt Brace Jovanovich.

Yood, H. 1996. Personal correspondence, March 17.

Young, R. E. 1978. "Paradigms and Problems: Needed Research in Rhetorical Invention." In *Research on Composing*, eds. C. R. Cooper and L. Odell, 29–47. Urbana, IL: NCTE.

Index

activities. *See* editing activities
addresses. *See* Internet
America Online, 58
Andrews, Philip, 69
Angelicchio, Nicole, 4
arguments, pro/con, 25
Aspects [computer program], 111
association, principle of, 14

Baker, Carolyn, 9, 33
Benedict, Michael, 57
Blau, Sheridan, 19
block, 101
boldface, 101
booktalks, 96
brainstorming, 20–24, 38, 66
browsers, 86, 101
Bucaria, Robin, 2, 93–95
budgets. *See* computer(s)
Busy Teachers' Web Site, 92–93

Canham, Ruth, 65
cautions. *See* Internet
CD-ROM technology, 32–33
Chamberlin, Rebecca, 52
character development. *See* fiction
chat rooms, 86, 101
Christensen, Francis, 42
CINQ2 [computer program], 26
cinquain, 26
citations, for electronic sources, 91
clusters, webs, diagrams, and trees, 21–24
Cole, Carolyn, 92
collaboration, 51–68
  with computers, 9, 11
collaborative
  assignments, 64
  editing, 82–84

prewriting, 31, 64
revision, 47–49
Collaborative Writer [computer program], 111
college applications. *See* Internet
Colomb, Gregory, 79
comments
  distinguishing, 55
  in text, 54
commercial web sites, 91
common disk posting, 60
Common Space [computer program], 110
community of writers, 62
CompuServe, 58
computer labs
  design of, 6–11
  equity, 7–8
  use of, 2–4, 6-8, 11
computering, defensive, 5
computer(s)
  and changing attitude about writing, 1–3, 10
  as electronic typewriter, 1
  budget for, 5
  literacy, 4
conclusions, 45–47
Conference on College Composition and Communication (CCCC), 96
  CCCC Bibliography of Composition and Rhetoric, 97
  CCCC Online, 97
Conference Writer [computer program], 59
conferencing, 51–68
conversation, directed, 64
copy/move sequence, 17, 20, 25, 101
copying over, 19, 36, 41
correctness, reading for, 70

123

Index

Cosgrove, Neil, 60
Cowden, Jane, 3, 52
credibility issue, 90
Crouse, Jamie Sue, 33, 69, 75
cyberspace, 86
Cyberwriting, 93

Daedalus Bibliocite [computer program], 113
Daedalus Classmanager [computer program], 111
Daedalus Interchange [computer program], 112
Daedalus Invent [computer program], 107
Daedalus Mail [computer program], 112
Daedalus Respond [computer program], 110
Derrick, Thomas, 31, 64
desktop publishing, 66, 81–82
Devil's Advocate, 24–25
diagrams, trees, cluster, and webs, 21–24
dictionaries, 71
distance learning, 98
Documentation Hotline [computer program], 113
Dzendzel, Kelly, 71

E-mail (Electronic mail), 52, 65, 87, 95, 102
Edds, Carolyn J., 92
Edit! [computer program], 114
editing, 35, 69–84
editing activity
  punctuation, 82
  replace-the-verb, 83
  replace-a-pronoun, 84
Editor [computer program], 114–115
Elbow, Peter, 14, 15, 16, 64
electronic
  bulletin board, 95
  literary magazine, 96
  professional journals, 97
equity, 7–8

extra sentence editing activity, 83

FAQs (frequently asked-questions), 89, 102
fiction, character development in, 67
file(s)
  duplicating, 41, 49
  extensions, 102
  guidance, 27
  importing, 103
  lesson, 27
  renaming, 39, 41, 49, 55, 60, 105
  response, 63
  saving, 105
  servers, 58, 102
Fine Lines [computer program], 107
five w's, 27
fixation and rigid rules, 37
Flower, Linda, 16, 47
freewriting, 14–15
functional sentence perspective, 79
fuzzy words, 80

generate-then-judge strategy, 13, 16
Golub, Jeff, 1, 83
Grammatik 5 [computer program], 115
Grampop [computer program], 115
Great Punctuation Game, 82
group opinion postings, 65
Gunning Fog index, 75
Guth, Hans, 36

Haas, Chris, 69
Hackett, Joseph, 26
hard copy, 102
Hartwell, Pat, 82
Hawisher, Gail, 97
Hayes, John, 69
Heide, Ann, 3
Heinemann-Boynton/Cook, 92
Henderson, Dale, 3
Heyn, John, 84
Higher-Order Concerns (HOCs), 36, 69
home pages, 86, 88, 89, 102

124

Index

Howard, Tharon, 96
hyperspace, 86
hypertext markup language (html), 93–94, 102, 103
hypertext transfer protocol (http://), 87, 103

I-Search Paper, 94-95
ideas
  generating, 13–34
  organization of, 20
information
  highway, 86
  resources, 95
Inspiration [computer program], 24, 108
Instructional Technology committee, 96
interface cards, 58
Internet, 58, 85–99
  addresses, 86
  cautions, 88
  college applications, 96
  conference groups, 95
  exchanging writing on, 93
  on-line courses, 98
  professional organizations, 96
  transactions, 88
introductions, 45–47
invention, 13–34

Jago, Carol, 4, 11, 95
James-Catalano, C. N., 90, 93
Java languaging program, 87, 103

keyboard exchange, 64
Kiernan, Henry, 7, 57
King-Shaver, Barbara, 2, 3
Kohrman, Cordelia, 96

LAN (local-area network), 57, 59, 103
Lanzoni, Sandra, 4, 10, 67
Learning Tool [computer program], 108
learning, computer view of, 99

LeBlanc, Paul, 25
links to other sites, 89, 103
listing, invention strategy, 20
listservs, 98
log on, 103
Lower-Order Concerns (LOCs), 69

Macrorie, Ken, 94
Marcus, Stephen, 18, 19, 31, 64
Marinos, Justin, 71
McAndrew, Donald, 9, 36, 69, 99
merging comments, 55
Microsoft Network, 58
modem, 58, 104
Monahan, Brian, 97
MOO (MUD, Object-Oriented), 97, 98, 104
Morrison, Laurie, 28
mouse, 104
move, 101
MUD (Multiple-User Dimension), 86, 98, 104
Murray, Donald, 46

National Council of Teachers of English, 58, 96
Native American Information Resource Server, 92
navigators, 86, 104–105
network, 31, 105
Nota Bene [computer program], 113
notepad, 59
nutshelling, 15–18

online
  professional conference, 97
  courses through Internet, 98
  job search, 97
  professional journals, 97
  research, 97
outlining, 37–40
  post-facto outline, 38, 48
ownership, psychological, 53

paper exchange, 51
Paradigm On-Line Writing Assistant, 108–109

Index

paragraphing
  as a revision activity, 44–47
  inserting breaks, 48
  length, 43
  making new, 43–45
  rearranging, 48
  reformatting, 43
parental concern, 88, 93
Paterson, Wendy, 41
Pedersen, Elray, 82
Persin, Diane, 33, 72
Pirate [lesson file], 28–30
Porter, Wanda, 15
posting
  group opinion, 65
  messages, 59
  to a common disk, 60
prewriting, 10, 13–34
privacy issue. 93
Pro-Cite [computer program], 114
Prodigy, 58
projector, overhead, with LCD panel, 66
protocol
  reading, 63
  turn-taking, 60

QUEST [computer program], 25–26
questions for response, 62

readability index, 74
reader feedback, 52–53
reader-friendly, 70
reading
  for correctness, 70
  protocols, 63
Realtime Writer [computer program], 112
Reigstad, Thomas, 36, 69
Research Helper [computer program], 114
revision, 35–49
  cosmetics of, 36
  global, 49
  idiosyncratic strategies for, 37
rhetoric, generative, 42

rhetorical
  invention, 10, 13–34
  prompt, 25, 27
risk-taking, compensation for, 18
Roberts, David, 59
Rodrigues, Dawn and Ray, 27, 55
Romas, Kristi, 73
Rose, Mike, 37

Schenkenber, Mary, 66
Schriver, Karen, 63
Schwartz, Helen, 43, 60, 96
scrolling, 105
search engines, 87, 92, 95, 105
search-and-replace, 56, 79, 80, 105
Sebastiani, Lee, 67
SEEN [computer program], 60, 110
Selfe, Cindy, 96
sentence separation, 41–42, 48
  as editing strategy, 78
sentence-combining techniques, 43
sentences, cumulative, 42–43
Shaver, J. P., 4
signature symbol, 55–56
Simmons, Kathy, 8, 9–10
slot-and-fill poetry, 26
Smith, Frank, 99
software
  collaborative revision, 110–111
  document research, 113–114
  generate ideas, 107–109
  network collaboration, 111–113
  style analysis, 114–116
sound card, 105–106
spell checkers, 71, 72, 79
split screen, 21, 24
St. Michel, Terrie, 2, 3, 4, 8, 9, 60
Stewart, Katie, 4, 71, 73
Storyspace [computer program], 109
Strickland, Don, 91
Strickland, Ken, 44, 56
student-centered classrooms, 99
Stuver, Amber, 72
style checker, 73, 74, 76
Success with Writing [computer program], 109

126

Index

Takayoshi, Pamela, 61
talk-aloud protocols, 63
text
    generation of, 13–34
    modeling response to, 61
    response to, 61
    teaching response to, 61
thesaurus, 72
to be verbs, 77
transactions. *See* Internet
trees, clusters, webs, and diagrams, 21–24

URL (Universal Resource Listing), 86, 106

virtual, 106
    classroom, 98
    credibility, 43

Walker, Melissa, 91
Wallace, Ann, 21
Web page, 89
webs, diagrams, trees, and clusters, 21–24
whole class brainstorming, 66
wide-area network, 57, 106
Williams, Joseph, 79
windowing, 21, 24, 40–41, 55, 59, 63, 106
word wrap, 43
World Wide Web, 87, 106
Writer's Helper [computer program], 109
Writer's Workbench [computer program], 115–116
writing
    invisible, 19–20, 31
    process approach to, 11
    workshop, 3

Yood, Herbert, 5, 8, 9, 61